# Third Space, Information Sharing, and Participatory Design

# Synthesis Lectures on Information Concepts, Retrieval, and Services

Editor

**Gary Marchionini**, *University of North Carolina, Chapel Hill*

*Synthesis Lectures on Information Concepts, Retrieval, and Services* publishes short books on topics pertaining to information science and applications of technology to information discovery, production, distribution, and management. Potential topics include: data models, indexing theory and algorithms, classification, information architecture, information economics, privacy and identity, scholarly communication, bibliometrics and webometrics, personal information management, human information behavior, digital libraries, archives and preservation, cultural informatics, information retrieval evaluation, data fusion, relevance feedback, recommendation systems, question answering, natural language processing for retrieval, text summarization, multimedia retrieval, multilingual retrieval, and exploratory search.

Third Space, Information Sharing, and Participatory Design
Perben Hansen, Ina Fourie, and Anika Meyer

ISBN:978-3-031-01199-3  print
ISBN: 978-3-031-02327-9 ebook
ISBN: 978-3-031-00234-2 hardcover

DOI 10.1007/978-3-031-02327-9

A Publication in the Springer series
*SYNTHESIS LECTURES ON INFORMATION CONCEPTS, RETRIEVAL, AND SERVICES*
Lecture #74
Series Editor: Gary Marchionini, University of North Carolina at Chapel Hill

Series ISSN  1947-945X  Print  1947-9468  Electronic

# Third Space, Information Sharing, and Participatory Design

Preben Hansen
Department of Computer and Systems Sciences, Stockholm University, Sweden

Ina Fourie and Anika Meyer
Department of Information Science, University of Pretoria, South Africa

*SYNTHESIS LECTURES ON INFORMATION CONCEPTS, RETRIEVAL, AND SERVICES #74*

## ABSTRACT

Society faces many challenges in workplaces, everyday life situations, and education contexts. Within information behavior research, there are often calls to bridge inclusiveness and for greater collaboration, with user-centered design approaches and, more specifically, participatory design practices. Collaboration and participation are essential in addressing contemporary societal challenges, designing creative information objects and processes, as well as developing spaces for learning, and information and research interventions. The intention is to improve access to information and the benefits to be gained from that. This also applies to bridging the digital divide and for embracing artificial intelligence. With regard to research and practices within information behavior, it is crucial to consider that all users should be involved. Many information activities (i.e., activities falling under the umbrella terms of information behavior and information practices) manifest through participation, and thus, methods such as participatory design may help unfold both information behavior and practices as well as the creation of information objects, new models, and theories. Information sharing is one of its core activities. For participatory design with its value set of democratic, inclusive, and open participation towards innovative practices in a diversity of contexts, it is essential to understand how information activities such as sharing manifest itself. For information behavior studies it is essential to deepen understanding of how information sharing manifests in order to improve access to information and the use of information.

Third Space is a physical, virtual, cognitive, and conceptual space where participants may negotiate, reflect, and form new knowledge and worldviews working toward creative, practical and applicable solutions, finding innovative, appropriate research methods, interpreting findings, proposing new theories, recommending next steps, and even designing solutions such as new information objects or services. Information sharing in participatory design manifests in tandem with many other information interaction activities and especially information and cognitive processing. Although there are practices of individual information sharing and information encountering, information sharing mostly relates to collaborative information behavior practices, creativity, and collective decision-making.

Our purpose with this book is to enable students, researchers, and practitioners within a multi-disciplinary research field, including information studies and Human–Computer Interaction approaches, to gain a deeper understanding of how the core activity of information sharing in participatory design, in which Third Space may be a platform for information interaction, is taking place when using methods utilized in participatory design to address contemporary societal challenges. This could also apply for information behavior studies using participatory design as methodology. We elaborate interpretations of core concepts such as participatory design, Third Space, information sharing, and collaborative information behavior, before discussing participatory design methods and processes in more depth. We also touch on information behavior, information practice, and other important concepts. Third Space, information sharing, and information interaction are discussed in some detail. A framework, with Third Space as a core intersecting zone, platform, and adaptive and creative space to study information sharing and other information behavior and interactions are suggested. As a tool to envision information behavior and suggest future practices, participatory design serves as a set of methods and tools in which new interpretations of the design of information behavior studies and eventually new information objects are being initiated involving multiple stakeholders in future information landscapes. For this purpose, we argue that Third Space can be used as an intersection zone to study information sharing and other information activities, but more importantly it can serve as a Third Space Information Behavior (TSIB) study framework where participatory design methodology and processes are applied to information behavior research studies and applications such as information objects, systems, and services with recognition of the importance of situated awareness.

## KEYWORDS

Third Space, information behavior, information objects, information practice, information sharing, participatory design

# Contents

# List of Figures

# List of Tables

# Preface

Society faces many challenges in workplaces, everyday life situations, and education contexts. Calls to bridge inclusiveness and collaboration are often noted with user-centered design approaches in Human–Computer Interaction (HCI) and, more specifically, participatory design (PD) as a method to address such concerns (Allin et al., 2018; Aytekin and Rızvanoğlu, 2019; Buchmüller et al., 2011; DiSalvo et al., 2017; Simonsen and Robertson, 2012). The need for participatory design and its value in a diversity of contexts ranging from education, design, under-represented populations and communities, to health and research where people face intense demands for involvement and growth to a greater good, has been well argued (Falconer, 2014; Muller and Druin, 2012; Postavaru, 2014; Simonsen and Robertson, 2012). Collaboration and participative approaches are essential in addressing challenges, designing creative artifacts and processes, developing learning spaces and information and research interventions. It is beneficial if all relevant users and stakeholders could be involved. Information activities (i.e., information behavior activities) manifest during many different contexts and situations, also within participatory design activities. Information sharing and other information interaction activities (Bessant, 2009) are especially important and contribute to all phases of participatory design as well as individual and group constructivist evolvement and growth in a (Third) Space of collaboration. It is therefore essential to understand *Third Space* as a framework and a platform for studying *information activities*, such as information sharing, collaboration, and communication (Wagner and Ikas, 2008) and to distinguish it from information grounds that are widely acknowledged in information behavior research. This can further be supported by participatory design which is an approach to design and design practice and developing information entities and information objects, artifacts, or information services (such as Digital Library systems), which entails a set of methods and techniques. Relatively few studies have reported on information behavior and information sharing and participatory design (exceptions being Keshavarz, 2008; Meyer et al., 2018; Muller and Druin, 2012; Nickpour et al., 2014).

Participatory design is an approach to design and design practice that entails a variety of methods and techniques as well as cognitive processes such as collective reflection and understanding in complex contexts and environments, using appropriate tools and techniques to actively engage diverse communities (i.e., end-users and stakeholders) in creatively designing technologies, tools, products, information objects, environments, and businesses which are more responsive towards different socio-cognitive experiences, tasks, and domains. Methods utilized in participatory design are focused on engaging, understanding, and exploring different needs and goals of the people involved, as well as delivering products that reflect the needs of users, the shared understanding of stakeholders, and the values and emotional investment of stakeholders. Participatory design may facilitate creative processes and is marked by striving for clarity of coherent visions, goals and needs, and socially sensitive perspectives (DiSalvo et al., 2017; Kang et al., 2015; Parviainen et al., 2017; Simonsen and Hertzum, 2012; Simonsen and Robertson, 2012).

A participatory design team can encompass and involve stakeholders and end-users from all levels of expertise, backgrounds, age groups, and cultures as stakeholders potentially contributing to all phases of developing a technology, a procedure, or a design activity. In this manuscript, our argument will be that both (a) participatory design as an approach that can address contemporary societal challenges and that involves a diversity of stakeholders, and the (b) information interaction activities—specifically information sharing activities—that manifest in the application of this method, are utilizing a place or space (Third Space) in which to discuss problems, find new solutions, gain new knowledge, and adapt world views.

Our interpretation of Third Space as framework build on interpretations from Human–Computer Interaction, participatory design, and guided inquiry (information literacy) (Kuhlthau and Cole, 2012; Kuhlthau et al., 2015; Maniotes, 2005; Meyer et al., 2018; Muller and Druin, 2012). Third Space refers to a fertile environment in which participants can relate, understand, and combine diverse knowledge into new insights and paths for action, thinking, and problem-solving. Such a space may have important attributes which include challenging assumptions, learning reciprocally, creating new ideas and solutions; these emerge through negotiation, co-creation, communication, information sharing, and other information activities.

This lecture will present Third Space as framework supported by participatory activities as: (a) an approach that can address contemporary challenges in a diversity of contexts, with a diversity of evolving and contributing participatory stakeholders; (b) as an approach that requires an intersectional zone where a diversity of information activities such as information sharing, information encountering, articulation of needs and other information interactions, manifest and that contribute to stakeholders' evolvement and contribution; and (c) an approach that can be used in information behavior and information practice studies.

The target audience is students, researchers, and practitioners with an interest in the practice of participatory design and the manifestation of information interactions, whether coming from information sciences, Human–Computer Interaction or a related discipline.

In Chapter 1, we introduce the challenges faced in contemporary society, sketching the emphasis on collaboration, inclusiveness, creativity, and innovation. We present the participatory design approach as an approach to address these contemporary challenges as well as Third Space as a framework for the space in which activities, the evolvement of knowledge and worldviews, will manifest, and information sharing and information interaction as core information activities. In Chapter 2, we call on some concepts to argue our points such as participatory design, Third Space, information sharing, co-creation and co-design, information sharing, and other related terms.

Chapter 3 presents participatory design as an approach and includes discussions on a synthesis of participatory design models, frameworks, and theoretical foundations. In Chapter 4, we discuss Third Space as a concept relevant to Human–Computer Interaction and participatory design, as well as information behavior (which embraces literature on guided inquiry and information literacy). In Chapter 5, we delve into the concepts of information sharing, information encountering and other information interaction activities to study them through various lenses such as information behavior and information practice. Chapter 6 presents a discussion on Third Space as a framework for participation and the manifestation of information sharing activities in Third Space as an *intersecting zone*. In this chapter, we also present our own suggestion for a Third Space information behavior (TSIB) study framework for information behavior research supported by participatory processes. The way forward including suggestions for practice and further research is provided in Chapter 7.

The TSIB framework can be used in studies of information behavior, the creation of objects and in creativity, specifically information behavior studies that can improve information services and interventions (Fidel, 2012; Hepworth, 2004, 2007). The value of Third Space is that it allows people to informally share information, connect and synthesize the information to come to new understandings. The intention with the TSIB study framework is to enrich information behavior research to do work with a wider group of participants and innovative methods of stimulating information sharing. The framework can furthermore encourage both students in disciplines such as information science and Human–Computer Interaction and experienced researchers to experiment with a new approach.

Preben Hansen, Ina Fourie, and Anika Meyer, 2021

# Acknowledgments

We are grateful to the many colleagues, local and international, who have contributed to this work in various ways, particularly Morgan & Claypool series editor Professor Gary Marchionini, Morgan & Claypool staff members Diane Cerra, Melanie Carlson. We also want to thank Dr. Elisabeth Sanders, and Professor Pieter Jan Stappers for kind permission to use images in this book. We would also like to thank Dr. Ola Knutsson for reviewing selected chapters, Ms. Wilma Singleton for her kind help with the references, and an anonymous reviewer for valuable feedback.

# Abbreviations

| | |
|---|---|
| 3D | Three-dimensional |
| 4IR | Fourth Industrial Revolution |
| AI | Artificial intelligence |
| AR | Augmented reality |
| ASIS&T | Association for Information Science and Technology |
| CIB | Collaborative information behavior |
| CIS | Collaborative information seeking |
| HCI | Human–Computer Interaction |
| IB | Information behavior |
| ICT | Information and communication technology |
| ICU | Intensive care unit |
| IoT | Internet of Things |
| IR | Information retrieval |
| ISIC | Information seeking in context |
| GID | Guided inquiry design |
| ISP | Information search process |
| MR | Mixed reality |
| PD | Participatory design |
| QR | Quick response |
| TSIB | Third Space information behavior |
| VSD | Value sensitive design |
| VR | Virtual reality |

CHAPTER   1

# Introduction: Contemporary Challenges Faced in the Emerging Information Context

Humanity faces numerous environmental, social, and economic challenges in diverse contexts related to climate change, deforestation, water and food security, poverty, gender inequality in education, terrorism, human trafficking, fostering ethical market economies, global health, and fighting new as well as re-emerging diseases. Furthermore, these challenges are impacted by the rapid pace at which digitalization and technological developments have been taking place over the last 20 years.

> *At the end of the 20th century, the watchword was globalization, which represented the breaking of barriers between countries. Now, in this 21st century, we are experiencing the digital age in which information transits at instant speed and there is direct communication between people, without time and space limits* (Belluzzo and Rosetto, 2021, p. 1).

While these technological developments could advance our present standard of living, there is a greater chance that they could also exacerbate the adverse and often unintended implications of new technological developments brought on by the Fourth Industrial Revolution (4IR). The precise impact of this revolution and other evolutions to come for commerce, government, healthcare and education remain unknown. However, one thing is certain—as technology evolves, so does the need for society to prepare and adapt to emerging technologies to succeed in a rapidly changing world. There are many cases, specifically related to information technology, where people from different contexts and disciplines are collaborating to find the best solutions, for example, designing information and communication technologies to support sustainable agricultural development (Kendall and Dearden, 2018); designing and developing an electronic tool to advance interprofessional communication and collaboration among frontline clinicians (Tang et al., 2018); and co-designing a suite of mobile learning tools for nursing students to support their learning experience and overcome their theory-practice gap (Egilsdottir et al., 2021). Emerging technological advances such as artificial intelligence (AI), mobile supercomputing, cloud technologies, Internet of Things (IoT), and intelligent robots have escalated to such a point that it has triggered a digital transformation (Schwab, 2017; Stein et al., 2016). This transformation is reshaping humanity's behavior in the way we work, live, communicate, and use information effectively, as well as the skills, abilities, and knowledge required to use emerging technologies for daily tasks. This need to quickly adapt has worsened the challenges mentioned above and subsequently created additional contemporary challenges such as inequalities, social justice, fairness, insecurity, gaps in skills, exclusion of minority groups, and increasing demand for societies to keep up with the pace of technological changes to ensure they do not fall victim to the digital divide (Ballantyne et al., 2017; Manda and Dhaou, 2019; Maynard, 2015; Postelnicu and Câlea, 2019; Xu et al., 2018). This increased the need for collaboration (Egilsdottir et al., 2021; Priya, Shabitha, and Radhakrishnan, 2020).

In the section to follow, we sketch these challenges in more detail as background for the emerging contemporary context that necessitates a better understanding of people's information activities, how they share and interact with information (thus, information behavior), as well as the use of participatory methods (such as participatory design), to collectively and collaboratively find solutions to complex problems and tasks.

## 1.1    THE PRESSURE TO KEEP UP WITH THE PACE OF TECHNOLOGICAL CHANGES

Organizations are under constant pressure to change and stay current, think critically and creatively, collaborate with others, and communicate, use, and share information to solve complex tasks in a world where technology evolves rapidly. Particularly, they need certain skills to interact and use various types of information in the digital age. Therefore, information literacy skills are of great importance to ensure that individuals have the ability to identify an information need, locate, make sense, critically evaluate, and effectively apply information to solve complex tasks in contemporary society—the fourth industrial age. But, it is important to remember that this digital transformation goes far beyond just operational, technological, and organizational changes; it also includes changes in the way individual's think, exist, act, as well as how they relate to people, feelings, things, attitudes and behaviors, and what is required for multi- and inter-disciplinary knowledge to collaborate in various activities in different contexts. There is a need to find innovative solutions; apply new research foci and research lenses (e.g., information behavior as a research lens) to increase collaborative and participative methods such as participatory design to address these challenges, to ensure change, and to find solutions. As a result, it requires a deeper understanding of individuals' information behavior and even more their information sharing activities (Hansen and Widén, 2017; Meyer et al., 2020). For instance, looking at information sharing as a core activity in collaborative work and learning to inform information literacy training. This can prepare people to deal with the challenges put by technological developments associated with digital transformation and probable other innovations that are not currently known. It might also enable intergenerational work and support, e.g., promote opportunities to learn new skills and transfer knowledge, expertise, and lessons learned (Rupčić, 2018). But for now, we should not get ahead of ourselves; this is for another day.

## 1.2    BRIDGING GAPS ACROSS SKILLS, KNOWLEDGE, CULTURES, GENERATIONS, AND DIGITAL (GAP) DIVIDE

The nature of work and the knowledge and skills required to complete work tasks have rapidly changed. So, individuals and organizations must renew, expand, and update their skills and develop new expertise and knowledge to be resilient. However, "there is a gap between the rate at which technology develops and the rate at which society develops. We need to take care not to fall into that gap," namely the digital (gap) divide (Vogels, Rainie, and Anderson, 2020, p. 109). As a result, efforts are needed to deal with the: (a) digital divide (information poverty and information inequality); (b) gap in information skills; (c) generation gap among individuals with different value systems, perspectives, and beliefs; and lastly, (d) limited understanding or gap in knowledge of the socio-cultural context in which the complex solutions are required.

(a) Global interconnectedness brought about by digital transformation has accelerated the "rise of connectivity," and therefore, communities facing issues of connectivity (both the cost and availability of network connection) and access to technology and computer literacy have become victims of the "digital divide." This term refers to the uneven access to/distribution of Information and Communication Technologies (ICT) in societies. This digital divide might exacerbate inequalities between the information-rich and poor. Consequently, information poverty can bring about information inequality generated by a lack of infrastructure needed to access knowledge and poor information skills.

(b) Poor information skills, specifically information literacy skills, could create barriers in accessing, understanding, evaluating, and interpreting information from various sources, resulting in ineffective communication, missed opportunities, suppressed innovation, conflict, misguided decisions, and the distribution of misinformation and mistrust. Good information skills and effective communication are also required to bridge generational gaps and to foster collaboration.

(c) Communities face broadening skills gaps, increased difficulties to support intergenerational dialogue and barriers in eradicating a culture of silo mentality (Freeman et al., 2020; Urick et al., 2017). This has signaled the necessity to establish an environment (space), a common ground, to bridge this skills gap, foster better dialogue and effective communication to close generational gaps, as well as promote collaboration. For example, creating a shared space to encourage intergenerational groups to collaborate during the planning of design projects, searching for solutions, and sharing expertise (Rupčić, 2018).

(d) Culture has a great influence on the conception of place (Ujang and Zakariya, 2015), and the same place might be perceived differently by people of different cultures. Thus, when designing for vulnerable or marginalized communities within a specific socio-cultural context, user involvement is particularly important, as the cultural gap between designers and the target group can be great (Barcellini, Prost, and Cerf, 2015; Reynolds-Cuéllar and Delgado Ramos, 2020). The design requirements, design needs, and design outcomes are related to the context and are directly derived from the participants within or related to that context (Reynolds-Cuéllar and Delgado Ramos, 2020). Consequently, understanding the complexities of the participants and the society they live in and showing cultural sensitivity is essential for enabling vulnerable or marginalized communities to have a positive design experience from which they can benefit. Information sharing is especially of great significance when people must find solutions collectively.

Overall, there is a need to bridge various gaps (i.e., skills, generational, culture, knowledge, and digital gaps) and challenges resulting from rapid technological, social, and economic transformation. Digital transformation, marking contemporary society, is about more than just technology-driven change; it is an opportunity to help everyone, including leaders, policymakers, creators/ designers, and people from all income groups and nations, to harness converging technologies to create an inclusive, equal, fair, and human-centered future.

## 1.3    SUPPORTING INCLUSIVITY, DIVERSITY, AND EQUITY: SOCIAL RESPONSIBILITY

Although there is a strong focus in the information context on equity, diversity, and inclusion, as well as the improvement of information access for disadvantaged populations, there is increased pressure and urgency within information behavior research to bridge the digital divide, promote democratic participation, and foster greater collaboration, with user-centered design approaches, to create innovative practices in a diversity of contexts. User-centered design approaches in the field of information behavior can be applied to understand users' social, physical and cognitive experiences related to their information needs as well as to understand their information activities during participation. In Human–Computer Interaction (HCI) and software design, a participatory design method can be applied to promote users' involvement in all stages of the design process to ensure systems fit their needs (Stein et al., 2016). In collaborative and participatory activities, various information interactions can manifest, and thus, methods such as participatory design may assist in gaining a richer insight into individuals' information behavior (e.g., information sharing), needs, and practices when creating innovative information objects as well as new models and theories.

It is becoming clear that Library and Information Science (LIS) specialists need to engage more effectively with and better identify their communities' information needs. More specifically, it is the social responsibility of Library and Information Science programs worldwide to integrate social justice, social equity, inclusion advocacy, critical information literacies, and to engage with scholarship while partnering with minority and underserved populations to make meaningful changes in the lives of their community stakeholders through their education and practice of information-related work. Policymakers in institutions, services, and corporate bodies must also recognize their social responsibilities and act accordingly to benefit society and its citizens.

The term *social responsibility* can be applied at both an organizational level (known as corporate social responsibility) and on an individual level (individual responsibility). Rogerson (2004) explains that corporate social responsibility can be described as an organizations' responsibility to promote social justice through fostering the view that everybody deserves equal economic, political, and social rights and opportunities; to improve society's participation, particularly for disadvantaged communities, through enhancing opportunities to access resources, voice their opinions, and build mutual respect and trust; and lastly, to acknowledge that their activities and actions have a social impact on people and communities.

It is crucial for modern organizations to address contemporary challenges and to make a *social impact* in the information environment of digital transformation. And even more, methods utilized in participatory design are required as well as understanding the various information activities arising to overcome these challenges. This necessitates collaboration with people from other fields, e.g., specialists/people in Human–Computer Interaction and Informatics that face similar responsibilities.

## 1.4     MAKING AN IMPACT: SOCIETAL IMPACT

Steinerová (2019), an information behavior researcher, highlights that the development of new services and tools shape the societal impact of information in terms of information use and advancement of understanding. Resultantly, to comprehend the social impact of information, we need to combine socio-technological, socio-cultural, and socio-cognitive contexts of information practices in which shared understanding, shared visions, and shared spaces dominate. More precisely, several researchers in the field of human information behavior (Case and Given, 2016; Greifeneder, 2014; Greifeneder et al., 2018; Vakkari, 2008; Wilson, 2018) established that societal impact is grounded on the development of information policies (e.g., regarding the digital divide), focus on the participation of special communities (minority or disadvantaged groups), technological development (social media), and adverse effects of information (e.g., disinformation, misinformation, information overload, and distrust).

Hence, establishing a positive societal impact implies that both academics and industry practitioners ensure that positive relationships and interactions are formed between organizations and their stakeholders. These social factors are unified in "a multidimensional conceptual space of social relations patterns, collaboration, information sharing, and adaptations" (Steinerová, 2019). And even more specifically, "finding the balance between individual and social values of information, manifold stratified information interactions and adaptations and cultivation of the information environment." In essence, we should explore the societal impact of information behavior studies linked to new social theories and participatory research methods to overcome societal complexities such as the digital divide, information poverty, misinformation, information overload, human indignity, discrimination, and inequalities related to access of information (Greifeneder, 2014; Greifeneder et al., 2018; Steinerová, 2019; Wilson, 2018).

It is the social responsibility of those involved in the planning, development, and implementation of emerging technologies, tools, and services to ensure that they consider the societal impact of their activities and actions and to involve diverse groups of individuals from various contexts actively (Steinerová, 2019).

## 1.5    HUMAN–INFORMATION INTERACTION AND FAIRNESS

Within the area of information searching and information systems, especially in information retrieval (IR), ranking and filtering has traditionally been evaluated based on relevance of search results to people searching for information, trying to deliver as correct results as possible to the right people.

Information systems are not developed in isolation. Neither are the information systems curated, managed, administered, and used in isolation. This has been recognized in the HCI community as well as in the participatory design community. The development and design of information systems characteristics, such as IR systems, clearly reflect the norms and values of those who designed the systems as well as the community and culture in which it has emerged. For example, Friedman developed a theoretically grounded approach (Friedman and Hendry, 2019) called value sensitive design (VSD), to the design of information systems that highlight human values and ethical values of stakeholders. Information systems, such as IR systems and digital library systems, shape the interaction between people and systems and information. This also suggests that search is not just a one-way activity, but increasingly people are getting searched. The system knows when and how and what the user searches for and can thus adjust as well as enforce the implications of those searches. You make yourself visible. Furthermore, it has been debated if information is accessible across different communities when it comes to if the information in the information systems covers information needs across all communities. For example, information needs of certain indigenous communities may not be supported.

This raises several important aspects that need to be addressed, like integrity issues, fairness, discrimination, and transparency. One way to address these phenomena is to utilize methodologies and tools that may allow people to express opinions and concerns when designing and developing information systems as well as the content. The importance of participation by people and stakeholders and the application of participatory tools and techniques may ensure a more fair, transparent, and non-discriminating search environment.

Considering the before-mentioned contemporary challenges, issues, and concerns have prompted us to look at alternative approaches. Furthermore, this need has been encouraged by the impact of digital transformation and other innovations to come on the rapid growth of increasingly complex technologies that are bringing together the physical, digital, and biological worlds. Collaboration can bring together people from different disciplines with diverse skills and make a difference from input from different occupations. Especially, creating innovative technologies and systems that support an extensive array of contexts and users can be challenging. Participatory methods such as participatory design (Scariot et al., 2012) have been recommended in HCI and software design. Although participatory design methods are useful for HCI and the design of technologies, participatory design is also guided by ethical principles, as it focuses on multi-cultural participation, democracy, equality, inclusion, and sharing (Van der Velden et al., 2014). This makes the methodology suitable for contexts other than HCI.

"Participatory design (PD) is interested in giving users a voice in technology design, not only with the aim of designing 'better' tools but also to enable and legitimate users to bring in their expectations, fears and concerns" (Stein et al., 2016, p. 69). It brings different stakeholders together to collectively share their experiences and contribute to the design's common goal (Simonsen and Robertson, 2012). Hence, providing the underpinning for building social relations, eliminating power dynamics, mapping knowledge and norms of behavior, as well as, revealing expectations and values to promote negotiation and democratic participation (Williams, 2013).

The value of participatory design to address contemporary challenges lies in its use as a method to provide appropriate participatory tools and techniques to actively involve and empower multidisciplinary users and communities (i.e., stakeholders) to design their own future technologies, tools, and work practices collaboratively and creatively (Scariot et al., 2012, p. 2702). Furthermore, this method is marked by striving for clarity of coherent visions, goals, and needs, and collaboration through information and knowledge sharing practices among stakeholders across disciplinary borders (Simonsen and Hertzum, 2012). Thus, there is a need to create a "symmetry of knowledge" (Fowles, 2000) among all the stakeholders involved. Many efforts have been made to understand better how people process new knowledge, transfer their knowledge, and adapt their knowledge on an individual level (e.g., the work of Kuhlthau et al., 2015) and then also in groups. Sarina (2018) highlights that individuals need to constantly renew, expand, and gain new knowledge, skills, and experiences to adapt to emerging technologies. Consequently, a shared space is needed to facilitate collaboration, mutual learning, creativity, and sharing of information, knowledge, expertise and experiences among multigenerational, multicultural, and multidisciplinary groups of individuals. This type of shared space is referred to as a Third Space.

The concept of Third Space has been used in various contexts ranging from education (Kuhlthau et al., 2015) to urban environmental design (Wohl, 2017) to HCI (Muller, 2007; Muller and Druin, 2012). But more specifically, it is of great value for studies focusing on participatory design methods and information sharing, as Third Space serves as a boundary-crossing, hybrid, fluid, and transformative space to promote the movement from theory to practice (Muller and Druin, 2012; Schuck et al., 2017). In addition, Third Space provides a boundary object such as an information object that forms the boundary region between domains (different groups) to collectively generate a shared space (Leigh Star, 2010). It is characterized as being fluid, flexible, creative, and multilayered and multidimensional. Moreover, the collaborative nature of Third Space empowers the crossing of intellectual borders literally, figuratively, or imagined (Williams, 2013) through participatory methods (e.g., participatory design) and participants sharing information, knowledge, and lived experiences (Tajvidi et al., 2018). Information sharing and interactions manifest in Third Space using participatory design tools and techniques (Jensen et al., 2019). The richness of such experiences needs to be captured in information behavior research. This will be covered in more detail in further chapters. We will also acknowledge related theoretical constructs such as information grounds.

Ultimately, this lecture investigates the following: (a) the value of using participatory design as a method and process to inform information behavior studies; (b) the significance of Third Space as an intersection and interaction zone to promote participatory activities, creative activities, and information activities, specifically information sharing as a core information behavior activity; and in conclusion, (c) moving from theory to practice, we present our own suggestion for a TSIB study framework.

CHAPTER 2

# Foundation and Components

In the Introduction, we set the scene for a world marked by increasingly complex and dynamic work tasks and problems, where collaboration is not only important but also necessary. We work both individually but also together in order to create innovative ideas in areas such as healthcare, education, and governance are more pressing, and exciting, than ever. To a great extent, these problems require that multiple stakeholders, in different ways, decide to come together and actively initiate collaborative tasks in order to improve the systems and services.

Dealing with information and encountering information as part of our daily life and professional work tasks in order to advance as knowledgeable human beings and to understand both dynamic people and activities by people, may be seen as spaces and situations that encompass possibilities for, among other things, creativity. The space, in which we may be introduced to, and where we elaborate, unfold, generate, and encounter information, do give unexplored possibilities for information cultivation, transformation, and creation. Our conceptualization will encompass how certain methods from areas within HCI, especially participatory design supporting information behavior may be the foundation and utilization for finding new possibilities and processes for both theoretical and practical purposes within an extended information behavior context and with reference in particular to Third Space. Third Space is characterized by information activities and in participatory design, with collaboration. It is conditioned by certain (not conclusive) information activities.

One major and vital point of departure is of course the notion of information, here in this book, we will consider and acknowledge Buckland's interpretation of information. Buckland (1991) offers three meanings of "information," namely "information-as-process," "information-as-knowledge," and "information-as-thing" that includes data, text, documents, objects, and events. In this book, all three are relevant. Information behavior is considered as a process but most importantly, we will reconnect to information as a thing especially as an information object.

In this chapter, we briefly present key concepts such as participatory design, Third Space, co-creation, and HCI, to argue our point. We will also present information related concepts: collaborative information behavior, information sharing and information interaction, information objects, and informational artifacts. These concepts underlie interacting with and sharing of information objects by means of collaboration and participation and establishing a Third Space in which creative information interaction can take place.

Furthermore, as can be seen in Figure 2.1, we illustrate the relationship between these concepts and components. Basically, the figure focuses on the interdisciplinary possibilities between certain areas of information behavior and Human–Computer Interaction, followed by examples such as collaborative information behavior (CIB) and participatory design as sub-areas within each of these areas respectively. We then join these two areas towards each other, converging into the main focus of this book, the Third Space, a space that facilitates information activities supported by design methodologies.

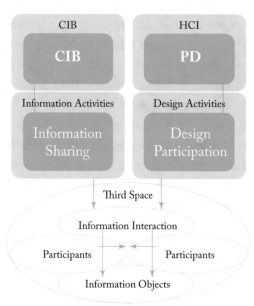

Figure 2.1: Relationships between major elements in this book.

We are presenting the concepts below in an order in which they connect in Figure 2.1.

## 2.1   COLLABORATIVE INFORMATION BEHAVIOR (CIB)

Collaborative information behavior describes information behavior that involves different people performing information activities together (Reddy et al., 2010; Ye et al., 2019). It falls under the umbrella concept of information behavior that is dealt with in more detail in Chapter 5 (cf., Section 5.2) and is key to the information activities in both participatory design and Third Space. Collaborative information behavior is an important area of research in the field of information behavior and information seeking. Within the research field of information seeking, researchers have pointed out the importance of the collaborative aspect (e.g., Foster, 2006; Hansen and Järvelin, 2005; Talja and Hansen, 2006) in both professional work situations as well as in everyday work.

Collaborative information behavior may include the formulation of information needs, seeking and retrieving of information individually or together, synthesizing and sharing information together, and the collective use of information among multiple people in a group activity. Karankunran et al. (2013, p. 2438) define collaborative information behavior as

> ...the totality of behavior exhibited when people work together to: (a) understand and formulate an information need through the help of shared representations; (b) seek the needed information through a cyclical process of searching, retrieving, and sharing; and (c) put the found information to use.

Furthermore, it has been proposed that people may have different motivations for and outcomes of collaborative information behavior, conditioned by different contexts in which collaborative information behavior occurs (Newman et al., 2015).

Collaborative information behavior activities have been examined in various organizational contexts such as healthcare teams (Reddy and Spence, 2008) and patent offices (Hansen and Järvelin, 2005) and educational settings (Hyldegård, 2006, 2009), with only limited work in leisure situations. Recently, studies within the tourism domain (Fardous et al., 2017; Mohammad Arif et al., 2015; Du et al., 2019; Ye et al., 2019) have tried to investigate and understand how and why people engage in collaborative information behavior when planning trips and traveling from an everyday leisure point of view.

Collaborative information behavior is a dynamic and complex phenomenon and underpins behavioral facets linked to each of the actors and the activity they are involved in and thus insights into the ways and patterns on how people act as individuals as well as in groups and how this needs to be supported. Collaborative information behavior involves multiple people, tasks and information activities and thus, it requires careful planning of collecting data, such as combining both qualitative and quantitative methods, it requires sensitive observations and questioning and complex handling of mixed data for the analysis work.

One observation is that collaborative information behavior may often occur when there is a breakdown in the information flow (Reddy et al., 2010). Reddy and Spence (2008) utilize a very interesting concept of "triggers," which they refer to as "...an event or situation within the environment that initiates collaborative information behavior amongst a formal or informal group of people..." (Reddy and Jansen, 2008, p. 78). Triggers then initiate a shift from individual information behavior to collaborative information behavior. For example, Reddy et al. (2010) report that triggers may be: (a) complexity of information need; (b) lack of immediately accessible information; (c) lack of domain expertise; and (d) fragmented information resources. One of the few collaborative information behavior models was also presented in Reddy et al. (2010) and Reddy and Spence (2008).

## 2.2    PARTICIPATORY DESIGN

Participatory design is considered as an approach and a process to design, attempting actively to involve both designers and stakeholders (such as end-users, customers, or employees) in the design process. The goal is to ensure that the design of a product, procedure, tool, system, or object meets the stakeholders' needs and is usable. The goal of practicing participatory design is to make the end-users, i.e., the consumers, part of the design process. Thus, they are seen as experts regarding their own needs, behavior, and views on everyday lives as well as work situations and as such, valuable partners in the design process. In contrast to user-centered design, that usually recognizes researchers and designers as being the experts and the people being served by design to be the subjects for the design and often only involved at the end of the design and the development process (Sanders, 2013).

The focus of participatory design is participation. Historically, participatory design was first introduced and applied in the American and Scandinavian quest for "democracy," "equality," and "participation" for systems design and the growing automation developments in the society (e.g., Ehn, 1989; Greenbaum and Kyng, 1991) claiming the positive and necessary effect of stakeholder involvement. Later, in North America, it evolved and then was named as co-creation. Today, participatory design has developed into a practical design method that tries to promote collective creativity and stakeholder involvement in many different situations, contexts, and domains as well as together with different user or stakeholder groups (Dalsgaard, 2010; Gullliksen et al., 1999; Yasuoka et al., 2013). According to Simonsen and Robertson (2012, p. 2), participatory design has been defined as:

> *A process of investigating, understanding, reflecting upon, establishing, developing, and supporting mutual learning between multiple participants in collective "reflection-in-action." The participants typically undertake the two principle roles of users and designers where the designers strive to learn the realities of the users' situation while the users strive to articulate their desired aims and learn appropriate technological means to obtain them.*

In its core elements, participatory design can be seen as a collection of tools and techniques, a set of methods, and a mindset (Sanders, 2013). In the design process, different participants are engaged in an interactive design process. Participatory design will be presented in more detail in Chapter 3. Figure 2.1 also depicts participants. Participants are further described in Sections 3.5.1 and 6.2 and design participation is mentioned in Sections 3.2 and 3.5.

## 2.3    INFORMATION SHARING

People commonly work and perform activities in groups and solve information problems in interaction with other people (e.g., Hansen and Järvelin, 2005). Given this background, collaborative information behavior (see Section 2.1) involving information sharing is emerging and is now also an established research direction (Hansen et al., 2015). Information sharing has been empirically studied in many contexts as an individual or group activity (Hansen and Järvelin, 2005; Harper, 1998; Harper and Sellen, 1995; Hertzum and Pejtersen, 2000; Marchionini, 1995; O'Day and Jeffries, 1993; Prekop, 2002; Sonnenwald and Pierce, 2000; Talja, 2002; Twidale et al., 1997).

The awareness of collaborative and sharing aspects in information seeking and behavior is not new and has been addressed during the last 15 years within different research disciplines. People often act in formal and informal groups while trying to solve different information seeking problems. In most human and agent-related situations (e.g., Internet of Things) sharing of data, information and knowledge (Savolainen, 2017) is a vital, natural, and instinctive activity. This is something we do in order to communicate so that we and other people can understand what we mean and how to advance knowledge and experiences in information handling situations.

Processes of collaborative information behavior may be deeply embedded in professional work contexts and other kinds of social, cultural, and professional practices. Information sharing is one such *dimension of social practices*. In this perspective, the social practice approach works from the assumption that all information seeking is social because all human practices are fundamentally social. This is, in turn, based on an understanding that (a) a common sense of what constitutes a practice is rooted "among members of a community of practitioners," rather than in the "heads of individual actors," and that (b) practices are usually organized in relation to other people in that community of co-workers, co-producers or customers. When information seeking is conceived as part of work practice or other social practices, the actors who search for and interpret information, whether individuals or teams are participants in a practice (Talja and Hansen, 2006).

As within research related to information behavior, the phenomenon of information sharing is widely diverse and may encompass different points of departure from different standpoints. Information sharing suggests that information may be shared both in a conscious or unconscious way with the purpose, or accidental intention to share information between two or more entities, humans, or agents (Savolainen, 2017). In information studies, information sharing can be understood as:

> ...*a set of activities by which information is provided to others, either proactively or upon request, such that the information has an impact on another person's (or persons') image of the world ... and creates a shared, or mutually compatible working, understanding of the world* (Sonnenwald, 2006, el.).

Importantly, Savolainen (2017) points out a *conceptual space* in which information sharing may take part. The most common view on information sharing is as a communication activity through which ideas, opinions, facts, and documents are transferred from an individual (or group) to other people (Savolainen, 2017). Hansen and Järvelin (2005) is one such empirical study showing this. The context (workplace) of patent engineers, established the conceptual space, in which the sharing of information happened. In this context, the sharing activity took place when the patent engineers stored representations (classification codes, query terms, and query strategies, and a short narrative of the problem). Furthermore, log-statistics indicating sources used, statistics on time and number of sessions, documents inspected, and documents written down and printed out and saved for future reuse by other colleagues. In addition, this information problem case was distributed and disseminated, by adding annotations to electronic versions of the documents. The annotations then served as a problem-solving use case for other colleagues.

The activity of information sharing behavior can be manifested as a collaboration between different entities of actors (such as humans or agents) with the purpose to achieve each individual's goal within the entity as well as the goals for the entire group. As such, a type of collaborative information behavior (cf., Section 2.1), information sharing is not an individual action but a collective and collaborative effort.

## 2.4    INFORMATION INTERACTION

Although used widely in the Information Science and Information Behavior literature, there is no precise consensus on the interpretation of information interaction. It is used with various information activities ranging from coming across information such as with information encountering, receiving information, consulting information sources including books and people, to social tagging. It is also often used with regard to human interaction with interactive information retrieval systems, e.g., for query formulation, displaying and verifying information, and work on intelligent information retrieval systems, distributed work environments, interaction with finding aids and information retrieval systems, receiving general guidelines and situated advice such as in counseling meetings with patients, task-based information interaction, search as learning and research related to learning and HCI (Eckerdal, 2012; Freund and Toms, 2016; Jank, 2010; Hansen and Rieh, 2016; Rieh et al., 2016). Fidel (2012), Marchionini (2008), and Park (2013) prefer the phrase human information interaction.

In their work with the information-based mitigation of intimate partner violence, Houston and Westbrook (2015) suggest a typology of information interaction limitations functions across a range of socio-economic contexts that lends itself to analysis of intractable power-based inequities. More systems-focused approaches such as Toms (2002) focus on what she refers to as the "'no-man's land' between user and computer articulating a model that includes user, content and system, illustrating the context for information architecture." Information interaction can be frequent or sporadic, formal or informal and may include what Olander (2007) refers to as social, collegial, and informational aspects and collegial interaction, as well as interaction with external sources. It can be dynamic and multidimensional (Park, 2013).

We acknowledge both the technological, artifacts, and human components in information interaction. Based on the work of Marchionini (2008), we interpret information interaction in line with the development of digital technology, changes in the nature of information and people's interaction with diverse forms of information, information sources and groups of people and technologies. According to Marchionini (2008, p. 165), "human-information interaction shifts the foci of all aspects of information work; blurs boundaries between information objects, technology, and people; and generate new forms of information."

Information interaction includes all activities where humans interact with information sources and systems that may include other humans, information systems, or devices, in a variety of formats involving diverse forms of information. Information sources can range from very traditional print books or other informational objects or artifacts to highly sophisticated digital formats to individuals and groups. Information can range from factual to emotional, and activities from gaining, sharing, interpreting, analyzing, and evaluating to using information. Both the human and technological components of information interaction are important. More specifically, there has been a shift from the importance of "discrete elements of information toward an ecological account of human–information interaction" (Marchionini, 2008, p. 165).

## 2.5    INFORMATION OBJECTS

Marchionini (2008, p. 165) notes that the information field remains to advance rapidly as digital technologies "change the very nature of information and how people interact with each other and with information." It has been argued that information may have several properties. Landauer (1991) suggested that information is physical and according to Krzanowski (2020), information can be subsumed under two categories: information as an abstract concept and information as a concrete physical phenomenon. By "abstract," Krzanowski refers to something not existing in space-time as a physical object. Second, information is regarded as a concrete physical phenomenon (Krzanowski, 2020, p. 2) where concrete means existing in space-time as a physical object. As such, information can be quantified and, more importantly here, *used*. Generally, information may be associated, in some way, with form, structure, and/or organization and information as a concrete physical phenomenon, may exhibit properties, such as that it is observable and it can be manipulated and can be quantified or measured (Krzanowski, 2020). The boundaries between information objects, people and technology have changed and new types of information are created or generated (Marchionini, 2008). There are three classical elements of the information field, namely: (a) information objects (which can include articles, books, and other physical and digital records); (b) people who create, use, manage, and share the objects to create mental (cognitive) representations; and (c) the technologies that capture, manage, store, and transmit information objects.

"The term information object includes the intellectual products of information activity and the recording of real-world objects and events" (Marchionini, 2008, p. 166). This aligns with Buckland's (1991) notion of "information as a thing." Information objects have traditionally been constructed by people who map information in their bodies or mind into forms of expression corresponding to culturally significant representation structures. People often utilize tools and technologies to craft physical and digital information objects which can be stored in a physical or digital format, as well as, consumed or experienced in one or more forms of human usable expressions such as visual, tactile, and aural (Buckland, 1991, p. 354).

Marchionini (2008) preferred to use the term information objects instead of information artifacts in his study, since the more general term "object" acknowledges the growing range of products and services produced by future technologies or emergent in human-machine networks. Therefore, information objects differ from information artifacts since "the artifact is the physical printed document or digital file. An information object is the component 'objective' extracted from an artifact. It is defined by the user's need, and not by "content" (Jones and Nemeth, 2005, pp. 169-170). Last, Jones and Nemeth (2005) indicate the significance of artifacts (physical, digital, or cognitive) that are produced and utilized by multiple participants in collaborative practices.

In essence, information objects are the components of an artifact that represent the cognitive objective for use of the information. For example, each task represents a different objective, and each task also orients to a type of information artifact. Thus, first an information artifact (i.e., published abstract) is sought. This is followed by the intention (cognition) of locating an information object (i.e., the object of searching, the answer, or specification of interest).

## 2.6    THIRD SPACE

*Third Space* is a concept that has featured in areas such as the information literacy and guided inquiry literature; in the literature of HCI (Muller and Druin, 2012) as well as recently, in the area of creativity (Meyer et al., 2018). For the purpose of this book, we will be following the intersection of the two interpretations of Third Space related to information behavior and HCI and participatory design.

- **From information behavior:** Kuhlthau and Cole (2012, p. 1) define the Third Space as "an intersection zone between the school curriculum and the student's knowledge and ways of knowing, creating a dynamic conception of the learning space that involves the student's outside-the-classroom knowledge." Kuhlthau and colleagues (2015, p. 32) explain that a Third Space provides a particular kind of adaptable learning space where "students can construct new worldviews rather than having to take on the teacher's perspective or those mandated by the curriculum or textbooks."

- **From Human–Computer Interaction:** Third Space may be considered as a fertile environment in which actors and participants can relate, understand and combine diverse knowledge into new insights and paths for action, practical activities, and thinking (Muller and Druin, 2012). Such a space may have important attributes which include aspects such as challenging assumptions, learning reciprocally, and creating new ideas, which emerge through negotiation and co-creation (Muller and Druin, 2012).

In our context, the Third Space should be understood as a framework, a platform that describes as well as offer a fluid, flexible, conversational, creative, and multilayered and multidimensional environment for emerging information, learning, and participatory activities that can be approached in different ways, e.g.:

- Third Space understood from an information behavior lens aligned with guided inquiry and information literacy; and

- Third Space as interpreted in HCI and in participatory design literature.

Muller and Druin (2012) conclude that the use of Third Space (or hybridity as they also call it) has resulted in the development of useful methods and techniques for enhancing and promoting effective communication, group cooperation and alignment to a task, critical thinking, realistic applications, and innovation. In such a way, participatory design may foster discussions and reflections that may challenge and unfold assumptions, norms, and values.

## 2.7    SUMMARY

In this chapter, we bring forward a set of concepts we anticipate will have importance for the understanding of our approach in this book. The concepts come from the two areas focused on here: information behavior and HCI. They stand as pillars from which we depart when developing our Third Space information behavior approach. Furthermore, we call on these concepts related to interacting with and sharing of information and information objects as well as when studying the creation of information objects using participation and participatory methods establishing a Third Space in which creative information interaction can take place. These concepts will follow in the preceding chapters.

CHAPTER 3

# Participatory Design as an Approach for Participation

Participatory design is a specific design approach and is embedded in the larger design tradition of HCI. Participatory design is considered as an approach and a process to design, attempting actively to involve both designers and stakeholders (such as end-users, customers, or employees) in a design process. The goal is to ensure that the design of a product, procedure, tool, service, or system meets the stakeholders needs and is usable. Thus, the concept of participation is important.

Generally, user-centered design practices use an iterative design cycle involving a set of stages such as understanding, designing, developing, and evaluating interactive systems. This book discusses the importance of considering people and their unmet user needs and responding to these needs through design, rather than technology when designing interactive information systems (Kjeldskov, 2014). One of its strengths is that it utilizes iterative scoping and prototyping activities (Twidale and Hansen 2019) in order to move forward in contrast to the more linear "waterfall" design approach. One of these user-centered design approaches is participatory design with its origin in Scandinavia (Ehn and Kyng 1987; Bödker 2006), particularly emphasizing active involvement and engagement of target users and other stakeholders in the design process. The reason for this is to ensure as much satisfaction and usefulness as possible of the developed output. As mentioned before, this collaborative and cooperative design process is done by practicing a research process where all actors cooperate in an iterative way. Participatory design is originally an approach to design within the area of HCI but has been applied in many contexts such as in software design, architecture, product design, service design, community design, medicine, and for marginalized populations. Participatory design deals with creating tools, systems, and environments that are responsive to the users of these tools, systems, and environments.

## 3.1 A SHORT HISTORY OF PARTICIPATORY DESIGN

Participatory design has its roots in a combination of political, social, and emerging rights in the work-life for a more inclusive and democratic engagement of people in their civil rights, decision-making, and values. The movement that started off during the 1960s and 1970s when people, not only started to show engagement in the global politics and social development but started also to look closer to their own living and work-situations as a response to large-scale transformations of workplaces, for example, within the industries when new tools and new technologies and computerization was introduced. The goal was to involve workers and their employers to provide people with better tools and processes in order to empower workers so that they could perform their work in a better and more satisfactory way on the one hand and at the same time establish more effective and efficient work processes for the company or organization. This has been extensively described and reported in the literature (Gulliksen et al., 1999; Nygaard and Bergo, 1975; Robertson and Simonsen, 2012; Yasuoka et al., 2013).

## 3.2    PARTICIPATORY DESIGN IS ABOUT PARTICIPATION

Participatory design is a process where participants and stakeholders from appropriate sectors of the context targeted by the design, collaborate and contribute towards a common goal. One of the central considerations is that they need to overcome social, cultural, professional and communication barriers that might hamper the design and development process. In the process, stakeholders communicate, share information, and address the challenges they experience working in and moving through a space of activities where they construct new meanings and redefine interpretations of the goals of a participatory design project. Information, information objects, and information sharing are pivotal in coping with mixed experiences, visions, objectives, and motivations, constructing new meaning, bridging gaps in knowledge and differences in worldviews, and coming to new insights and paths of action.

Participation is a key concept in any design process, especially an important element in participatory design processes. Participation can happen in different ways and can contribute or open ways in connection to different parts in the design process. Bratteteig and Wagner (2016) expand on the concept by looking on participation from three dimensions (p. 465).

(a) **Participation of what?** This dimension deals with the depth of participation. One of the most important and strong parts of participatory design is the participation to create choices. Important is also the user participation in *selecting among different choices*. This can be done at different stages in the design process and could be difficult in different ways for the users. The next step of participation is to concretize the selections. Here the challenge is if the users have the capabilities or the possibilities to participate depending on the technical level, vision, and complexity of a design project. Here the users may contribute in the form of storyboards and mock-ups. Next, the "see"/evaluate part (Bratteteig and Wagner, 2016, p. 467) of designing is important and involves so-called making design moves. For example, when testing or probing an *emerging design in use* or in a specific situation and context, is important. As closer the design comes to the potential real use situation, the better influence can the participating users have on the design and how it will be used in context. This possibility to test/validate the design, using for example a probe, will allow the users to participate in their own design choices.

(b) **What shapes participation?** The influence of context. The contextual framing of the projects including the situations are framing the project. Structural elements of the project context may limit the possibilities and abilities to participate and make choices (Bratteteig and Wagner, 2016, p. 455). Other aspects may influence the participation such as the power and influence of different participating stakeholders may have on other participants. For example, in very large and complex settings, such as a healthcare organization, stakeholders with different occupations, professional backgrounds, educations and work tasks, will find many challenges to find common grounds and based on their experiences and perspectives. Another aspect is that choices or decisions can influence each other sequentially or recursively (Bratteteig and Wagner, 2016, p. 463). Sequential linkages characterize decisions where one decision leads to a series of others, either smaller ones ("nesting") or larger ones ("snowballing"). On the other hand, a decision at some specific point can in different ways affect the premises for the next upcoming decision or on other, related design issues in different ways. This shift in decision can be caused by effects such as evoking, merging, or due to learning.

(c) **How participatory is the design result?** This dimension is dealing with one of the core aspects of participation: increasing users' ability or "power to" influence the design. It is about if the artifact(s) resulting from the design process, supports their ways of, or if it gives them a voice in and influence on work or everyday processes, they will otherwise not find possible.

Design, and especially participatory design, are about ensuring that all people and stakeholders that will use the technologies, services, or practices may be extensively involved and play a critical role in shaping its design, functions, and procedures. The concept of practice is important in connection to participatory design:

> *Through practice we produce the world, both the world of objects and our knowledge about this world. Practice is both action and reflection. But practice is also a social activity; it is produced in cooperation with others. However, this production of the world and our understanding of it takes place in an already existing world. The world is also a product of former practices. Hence, as part of practices, knowledge has to be understood socially—as producing or reproducing social processes and structures as well as being the product of them.*

(Ehn, 1993, p. 6)

It is generally agreed that the stakeholders' commitment to the participatory design process is of critical importance (Gulliksen et al., 1999; Yasuoka et al., 2013). Participatory design is about the participation of end-users in a creative design process. This process can be about designing and shaping a specific service or object that they themselves will be using in their daily life, work-life in a specific community or an organization, or even on a national level. This creative process may also involve the design, development, and creation of information elements, objects, artifacts, and systems.

Participatory design has the potential for designing technologies that more closely align with the needs, behaviors, and tasks of the users. Participatory design as a social engineering strategy draws on the knowledge of potential users and involves them in the design. At the same time as individuals are involved in the design process, they are also representing a group of people and their opinions. As such, participatory design moves beyond individuals and moves into larger systems in which groups of people (e.g., end-users, stakeholders) and their collaborative interaction with technology, that also include social interaction, work tasks, and strategies, align with the goals and purpose of the work tasks or everyday life situations. Then, as a body of information and knowledge, about human and collaborative activities within a context, it can inform the design of systems and how to implement both technology and also procedures. A successful participatory process is a community of practice in the making (Brandt et al., 2012).

## 3.3   PRINCIPLES IN PARTICIPATORY DESIGN

One of the key elements in participatory design is, as mentioned, the participation. The possibility, ability, but also the necessity of being part of the creation and design of something that will be part of your everyday life, is both obvious and desirable. This could be through enforcing certain values in the design to executing the design itself using programming code and, e.g., three-dimensional (3D) tools (Li et al., 2019).

When initiating and starting a participatory design process, there are certain values involved, emerging from practical and societal needs and demands. Participation and democracy are core principles (Bratteteig and Wagner, 2012; Robertson and Wagner, 2012; van der Velden and Mörtberg, 2015), and constitutes the possibility to be involved and express ideas and opinions. Another such sensitive topic in design and development for information interaction is the possibility to have a say in the process involving design activities and decisions that enable *equalizing power relations* (Kensing and Greenbaum, 2012; van der Velde and Mörtberg, 2015). One of the core characteristics of participatory design is the participation of people involved in the process of design. They are often referred to as stakeholders. Together the stakeholders of the intended new system or service co-realize the needs and expectations from a diversity of experiences, ideas, and knowledge. The commitment to participate in joint practices to achieve an understanding and future vision incorporating these experiences and knowledge also put some demands on the stakeholders. Their very specific wishes, opinions, and visions may not be shared by others and thus, there may be a democratic and equal negotiation that may result in that a stakeholder has to make compromises. However, these collaborative practices, and in that way, the process of participatory design, may enable trust among the participants (van der Velde and Mörtberg, 2015). This also included learning processes (Reynolds and Hansen, 2018) since people involved in the practice have different backgrounds and experiences and based on a respectful relationship among the stakeholders, an understanding of other viewpoints on function and technology, may emerge. This includes not only those for whom the design is intended but also the designers. Further to the democratic practices, participation commitment, and equality of power, Kensing and Greenbaum (2012) also mention four guiding principles: mutual learning and alternative visions about technology (both mentioned above) and situation-based actions, tools, and techniques. End-users, participants, and stakeholders will be mentioned in Section 3.5.1.

**Mutual and shared learning:** One of the cornerstones in participatory design is that participants through their participation and sharing of their own experiences, knowledge, values and visions will establish a rich and collective understanding among the participants and the stakeholders. According to Kensing and Greenbaum (2012), participatory design is a value-centered design approach because of its *ethical* motivation, which is built on values. This ethical stand has been defined as the recognition of "an accountability of design to the worlds it creates and the lives of those who inhabit them" (Robertson and Simonsen, 2012, p. 5). Some of these values challenge traditional system design and how we usually anticipate how (information) objects and (information) systems are designed and developed.

## 3.4    FRAMEWORKS WITHIN PARTICIPATORY DESIGN

This section will not give an exhaustive review of all the different types of models and frameworks that have been deployed in participatory design, but a short background and the development and nature of these. There have been many interesting frameworks proposed for participatory design, and Teal and French (2020) describe both a set of linear and nonlinear models.

Linear models are described as a step-by-step approach of overlapping stages and activities. One such method is the process-oriented MUST method (Kensing et al., 1998). Another method that Teal and French mention is the *contextmapping* (van Rijn et al., 2006) that propose sequential stages such as preparation, sensitization, group sessions, and analysis. The EBCD PD model (experience-based co-design) within the domain of health care (Dimopoulos-Bick et al., 2018) is focusing more on improving services than design innovations. One recent framework, the MOVE framework, proposed by Akoglu and Dankl (2019), outlines four phases: meeting stakeholders, switching over roles, voice ideas, and evaluation. These stages are suggested to provide: (a) spaces to enable empathy among a group of diverse stakeholders; (b) a design workshop outline which enables common ground; and (c) ideas and thoughts on changing roles of involved people.

The nonlinear frameworks and models reflect the *iterative* nature of design projects and participation is represented as iterative cycles (Dittrich and Lindeberg, 2004). One of the focuses of participatory design is the purpose of activities and linking to project goals that can build and enable *meaningful participation* (Sanders and Stappers, 2008) taking the whole experience into account. Another model by Muller and Druin (2012) includes young participants which include different roles of the participants as user, tester, informant, or design partner. Iterative methods or frameworks usually allow for flexible usage and combinations of different methods, techniques, and tools.

As mentioned above, one of the more nonlinear frameworks that reflect the iterative nature of the design process is Sanders et al. (2010) proposing a framework that suggests different methods, tools and techniques and how and when to apply them during a (participatory) design session. One of the major characteristics of participatory design is its flexible and dynamic usage of different and additional (new) tools and methods that can be added and combined in the design process (Teal and French, 2020). Based on the specific purpose of participation (to design a service, an object, or procedure), the framework gives advice on tools and activities to be used in terms of the form that participation takes. The modes of participation may be aligned with the type of individuals or groups.

Sanders and Stappers (2008) suggest a co-design process that supports a holistic approach regarding what the participants will encounter and what experiences they will have. Incorporating these aspects ensure that there is meaningful participation between stages in the design process. Even though this model is practical to understand participatory design focusing on activities of collaborative design, it does not address how to create the conditions for these activities to take place (Teal and French, 2020). However, the model includes four main stages of pre-design, the generative stage, the evaluative stage, and the post-design stage (Figure 3.1).

Pre-Design       Generative            Evaluative            Post-Design

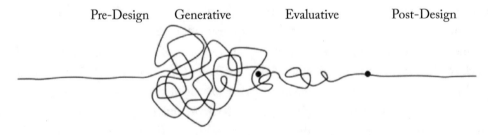

Figure 3.1: Design process. With special permission by Dr. Elisabeth Sanders. A variation of this can be found in Sanders and Stappers (2014).

This very descriptive and illuminative image of the nonlinear and winding road of the design thinking process, include a *pre-design stage* that focuses on the larger context of experience, expectations, and knowledges, while the *post-design stage* deal with how people actually experience the product, service, or space that was developed. The in-between two stages of *generative* (generating, producing, reproducing) design lead to different smaller and bigger design decisions, while the *evaluative stage* takes place during the subsequent design development process. The latter is labeled evaluative since the main goal is known and the prototypes serve as instantiations that provide the means for evaluation and subsequent refinement.

In the pre-design and generative stage (Figure 3.1) complementary and connected activities in co-designing are taking place. In Figure 3.2, Brandt, Binder, and Sanders (2012) describe the following activities: *making*, *telling*, and *enacting*.

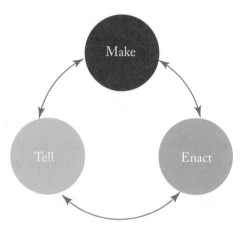

Figure 3.2: Making, telling, and enacting as complementary, connected activities in codesigning. With permission from E. Sanders. In: Brandt, Binder, and Sanders (2012).

Participatory design practices and activities entail tools and techniques that combine and facilitate telling, making, and enacting. Participatory design practices start at the beginning of the design process through prototyping activities involving the make-tell-enact model (Brandt, Binder, and Sanders, 2012). *Making*: through different materials, tools and objects, users can explore and elaborate ideas. *Telling*: describing or communicating an idea or vision can be done through telling. Methods used for describing an experience, an emotion, or knowledge can include methods like storytelling, dairies, documentaries, cards or movies. *Enacting*: involves scenario-making and envisioning and acting out and could also include role-playing in order to embody ideas, proposals, processes, and solutions.

## 3.5 EXAMPLE OF A PARTICIPATORY DESIGN WORKSHOP SETUP

The lead author has many years of experience in using different participatory design techniques and tools from several student and business projects. One such very typical participatory design set up is the Future Workshop approach (Jungk and Müllert, 1987; Kensing and Madsen, 1991). Initially,

Jungk and Müllert (1987) developed Future Workshops as a technique to empower and enable groups of people with scarce or limited resources to be able to contribute to the decision-making processes, especially of public planning authorities.

A participatory design workshop approach basically contains three stages, including: the preparation phase, the critique stage, the envisioning phase, and finally, the implementation stages, as depicted in Figure 3.4. Each of the stages can, depending on context and goal or purpose with the study, involve different activities that, in turn, actuate and utilize different tools and techniques in order to acquire data and information.

### 3.5.1    PARTICIPANTS, STAKEHOLDERS, AND END-USERS

The main goal and purpose of the design process are important when planning and applying a participatory design workshop (cf., Appendix A). A participatory design workshop may involve, depending on the purpose, 4–15 people in each group and may consist of several groups for a project depending on context and problem(s). Groups may be small groups and larger groups. This is to invite the end-users and stakeholders to elaborate, explore, and formulate, in an iterative way, from very loosely to more concrete ideas for solutions and design proposals.

Stakeholders are considered people that personally have an interest in the new tool, service, or system to be developed. For example, if the goal is to change a specific administrative information system within a global company, a participatory design workshop may be performed in each of the countries for which the company has offices in order to comply with different needs and work cultures. Furthermore, if the goal is to develop an economic administrative system, people within the economical department have a great interest so that the system is designed for their work purposes. Usually, a participatory design workshop is performed locally, with local participants. All persons taking part in a participatory design workshop or design process are considered as participants. These participants may be representatives for a group of users either with or without holding any stake in a design developed for a specific company (system, tool, or service). At the same time, stakeholders (professional role) can also be the end-user, and thus, a person can have several roles. The stakeholder is considering risks and benefits with the new design, among many things. One of the more critical aspects of participation in a participatory design process is that there is the notion that the "user" can play co-creating roles throughout the design process. Being part of the design process, i.e., becoming a "designer" may depend on the levels of expertise, and creativity of the "user," among other things (Sanders and Stappers, 2008). All people are considered creative human beings, but not all can become designers. Sanders (2006, p. 12) distinguishes four levels of creativity that can guide our thinking here: doing, adapting, making, and creating. People are living their daily lives engaged in multiple levels of creativity at the same time but at different levels. For example, while being at the creating level when writing up a report, you may at the same time be at the adapting level when it comes to understanding the use of the image drawing functions of that software technology. In this work, we will not go further into the area of creativity.

In addition, when taking part in a participatory design workshop design activity, they are considered as participants of the participatory design process. The important thing here is that it should be based on the participants' own experiences, knowledge, and creativity. The practical and applicability aspect is very important. During the process, design and technological proposals will emerge. They are usually related to a certain organization or community, a certain context, certain challenges or problems, both in relation to a local issue or challenge.

Participants may have different roles. Composing the group of participants is highly important and will affect the progress, process, and outcome of the creating activity such as a creative workshop. Participants generally represent different work occupations within a company, for example, if there is a new technology introduced to the company operations, different types of workers may be interacting with that technology in different ways. The participants may represent different ages and genders or may have different positions in a business. Moreover, roles can be defined according to the interaction, like interacting role, group-oriented role, task-oriented role, and production role (Barcelli, Prost, and Cerf, 2015). The researcher/designer can have different positions in the design activity. Researchers/designers may be part of the design process and the researcher may also be totally outside. There is a tension with how much a researcher should intertwine in the creative process. There is the issue of power balance and independence aspect to consider. So, the composition of the group could involve so-called champions, experts, leaders, and boundary spanners (Barcelli, Prost, and Cerf, 2015). As Halskov and Hansen (2015) point out, researchers need to be more careful and precise about who to bring into the design event and also think more about the users' roles when planning design events, selecting methods, interpreting and selecting design materials, and making decisions.

## 3.5.2 PROCEDURE DESCRIPTION

A participatory design workshop (such as the Future Workshop) incorporates, in general, a three-phased work process (Apel, 2004; Jungk and Müllert, 1987): a critical analysis of the current situation (the critique phase) which is used to frame and focus on the visions and future applications and utility of the design (the envisioning phase) and finally the assessments or evaluation phase is done to check if the initial goal and ideas are being followed and sets of proposals are suggested and implemented (the implementation phase). A participatory design workshop does not have a specific time limit but can last between several hours and up to several days. Three general phases are depicted in Figure 3.3.

> **Phase 1—critique phase:** The focus in this stage is given to a critical analysis of the current contextual, technological, situational, and design situation. The problem(s) is

investigated critically and in-depth jointly between all participants and stakeholders. Design methods that can be used in this phase are drawings, affinity diagrams, and thematic analysis. Different types of brainstorming can be used and problem-related critical questions can be framed.

**Phase 2—envisioning phase:** In this phase, all participants jointly work on future visions and possibilities and ideas. The important critical analysis in phase two forms the basis of one or several brainstorming sessions. These could involve different techniques like drawings, storyboards, and enactments in order to draft function and action proposals.

**Phase 3—implementation phase:** In the implementation phase, the ideas and proposals are assessed and critically evaluated in regard to, for example, their feasibility. In this stage, the proposals from phase three are further developed, now with an emphasis on more real-life applicability practices. A connection is made to the process phases of one to three in order to see if in the established context: (a) the problem(s) and goal(s) have been met and (b) if the vision and possibilities for all the participants have been involved and included. In this phase, a more concrete project is formed in which needs, ideas, and expectations are clarified and incorporated.

Figure 3.3: The three general phases in a general participatory design workshop (by authors).

### 3.5.3    ACTIVITIES WITHIN THE PARTICIPATORY DESIGN PHASES

More specifically, the following examples of activities may take place within the different phases of a participatory design workshop: the critique phase; the envisioning phase; and the implementation phase. Each of the phases can be broken down into smaller activities which may include data and information from the previous phase in an evolving and iterative design process. Figure 3.4 gives some examples of activities for Phases 1, 2, and 3. It also gives potential design methods such as focus group interviews and card sets (e.g., Sanders and Stappers, 2014).

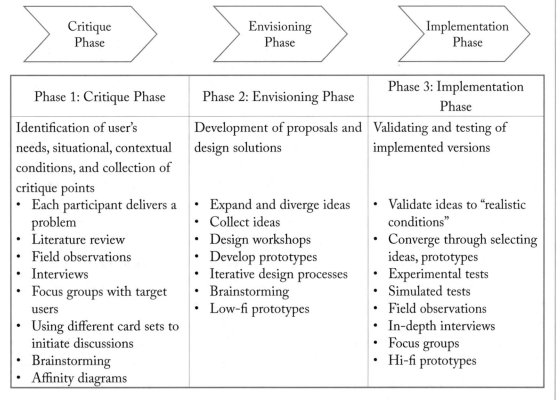

| Phase 1: Critique Phase | Phase 2: Envisioning Phase | Phase 3: Implementation Phase |
|---|---|---|
| Identification of user's needs, situational, contextual conditions, and collection of critique points | Development of proposals and design solutions | Validating and testing of implemented versions |
| • Each participant delivers a problem<br>• Literature review<br>• Field observations<br>• Interviews<br>• Focus groups with target users<br>• Using different card sets to initiate discussions<br>• Brainstorming<br>• Affinity diagrams | • Expand and diverge ideas<br>• Collect ideas<br>• Design workshops<br>• Develop prototypes<br>• Iterative design processes<br>• Brainstorming<br>• Low-fi prototypes | • Validate ideas to "realistic conditions"<br>• Converge through selecting ideas, prototypes<br>• Experimental tests<br>• Simulated tests<br>• Field observations<br>• In-depth interviews<br>• Focus groups<br>• Hi-fi prototypes |

Figure 3.4: Examples of design activities that can take place in each of the three steps of a design workshop.

Originally, the Future Workshop (Jungk and Müllert, 1987; Kensing and Madsen, 1991) was developed for different citizen groups or workers in organizations/companies who wanted a say in the decision-making process, for example when a new technology or a new work procedure was going to be introduced. Thus, a design workshop is suitable when for example new technologies will be introduced or changed and where the goal is to ensure that the design of this technology, procedure, or system meets the stakeholder's requirements, needs, and is usable. The focus of participatory design workshops could be a certain service or a specific function in a larger system. It could deal with elaborating specific scenarios to actually handling specific implementations of technologies and technology-based work processes related to a specific user population.

In Appendix A, we present a simple and general example of an information leaflet and outline preparing for a real-life participatory design exercise. This general outline has been utilized at different educational and professional (with companies) events in Sweden, the U.S., and China. In its core elements, participatory design can be seen as a collection of tools and techniques, a set of methods, and a mindset (Sanders, 2013).

### 3.5.4    CO-CREATION AND CO-DESIGN

Within the overall area of HCI, co-design is mentioned as a closely related design movement of human-centered design (HCD). A link between participatory design and co-design can be found in the work by Ehn (2008). He describes participatory design as design "with a special focus on people participating in the design process as co-designers" (2008, p. 93). According to De Koning et al. (2016), co-design can, therefore, be seen as a process used in participatory design. Furthermore, De Koning et al. (2016, p. 267) state that designers often describe co-creation as subordinate to co-design, since co-design is about the process of collaboration in which co-creation can take place. However, these terms have been widely used in different contexts and environments, both as a design practice and as theoretical constructs, and thus, there are a variety of definitions and no single established interpretation. Co-design can be understood as a creative practice, while co-creation is the co-making or the creative activity that makes something new emerge.

There has emerged a set of models and frameworks that give attention and focus on different aspects of design. Well-known and related design models like Stanford d.school design thinking model (2019) involve similar steps and stages such as: empathize, define, ideate, prototype and test and the Design Councils Double Diamond design model (Design Council, 2015) that involve steps like discover, define, develop and deliver. Another design thinking model developed by IDEO (2009) involves the following iterative steps: discovery, interpretation, ideation, implementation, and evolution. One of the common things reoccurring is a converging and diverging movement as the design process proceeds. Usually, the diverge phases include ideation and envisioning activities. For co-design and co-creation processes, De Koning et al. (2016) describe different types of co-creation models according to co-creation joint spaces, spectrum, types, and steps.

(a) **Joint space of creation:** These models generally consist of two circular entities with an overlapping space in between the two entities. In this space, the co-creation between the two entities is assumed to take place.

(b) **Co-creation spectrum:** These models show that co-creation is a phenomenon that takes place not only in the design field but also in other, related areas such as innovation, business production, learning, and participatory design. Here the space of creation can be seen along two axes and divided into a matrix, one that deals with the level of collaboration and the level of influence on the output. Furthermore, the spectrum also shows so-called "movements" (De Koning et al., 2016, p. 271), and they are (i) co-creation as a participatory design method and (ii) co-creation as an innovation approach.

(c) **Co-creation types:** In these models, De Koning et al. (2016), identified different levels of co-creation based on three criteria. They will result in different types of co-creation: (i) *when* along the design process the co-creation takes place; (ii) the *amount* of benefit or change there is for the co-creating end-user; and (iii) the *level* of collaboration between the different entities. Depending on how they unfold, they will result in different types of co-creation.

(d) **Co-creation steps**: Based on yet another set of different models, De Koning et al. (2016) identify and establish a set of steps to follow in a co-creation process: identify, analyze, define, design, realize, and evaluate. Furthermore, the design-step is broken down into smaller steps: invite, share, combine, select, and continue. According to De Koning et al. (2016), they should be deployed and practiced as a workshop. As can be noted, one of the design steps involved sharing (Figure 3.5).

These four aspects involving the space, the range, types, and steps of co-creation are relevant to the participative design process, once the creative activities are at hand. The four aspects all cover and entail a better understanding of a process in which something is being created.

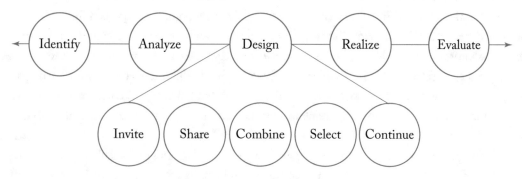

Figure 3.5: Five steps in a co-creation process. (After De Koning et al.'s [2016] five steps in a co-creation process). Authors' interpretation.

For a better understanding of how a creative space and process may function as well as being studied within an information behavior context, these described steps (Figure 3.5) may unfold important information behavior expressions, processes, and tasks. Using a practical approach of studying and unfolding information behavior activities and tasks might render new insights into ongoing and emerging information behavior processes. One of the interesting and major aspects from Figure 3.5 may, for example, be the design step which implies that we actually design information objects and how these can be studied. Other steps are known to the information behavior domain, such as analyzing and evaluating. The "design" step also shows that information behavior does not end with studying just the phenomena of processes and activities, but also that there is an outcome of information activities, creating new information objects, which, in turn, generate knowledge.

## 3.6   PARTICIPATORY DESIGN CHALLENGES

Participatory design has a clear social dimension in which the separate individual, as well as the whole, is equally important. The importance is that each member should ensure that the final product or service is developed and designed to fit the purpose of their specific (work) task or leisure activity. This perspective on the role of users in user-centered design is fundamental. The users are considered as "experts" in their own domain and the target for the proposed innovation. Since participatory design is focusing on people, their practices, needs, and expectations, and technologies, studies are more taking place as contextual inquiries, rather than in lab situations. Within participatory design the human user is a core element and elevates the user's needs and requirements and satisfaction. A major critique towards this type of design process is that it can only result in smaller (design) improvements. One reason for that is that the design process is heavily grounded in current practices and technologies (Kjeldskov, 2014). Another argument has been that users cannot be considered as good designers. They are experts in their own domains and context and may have the possibility to inform design, but their knowledge about technologies and design are limited. Furthermore, a recent article by Bødker and Kyng (2018) highlights challenges for participatory design in alignment to current local and global conditions and changes. Participatory design needs to adapt to new conditions and requirements and the authors suggest a new participatory design as they say "...*PD that matters*..." (Bødker and Kyng, 2018, p. 14). The core elements of this new participatory design approach are: (a) addressing areas where dramatic and potentially negative, changes are underway; (b) partner as major drivers; (c) researchers, in the dual role of being researchers and activists; (d) developing a vision for high and lasting impact; and finally, (e) safeguarding and developing the impact through democratic control (Bødker and Kyng, 2018).

## 3.7   SUMMARY

Participatory design is a design methodology consisting of a set of design tools and techniques in which different types of users or stakeholders participate as co-designers in the targeted design process. This design process may encompass both the current use and future use of a design (e.g., Wang et al., 2017; Parviainen et al., 2016, 2017). In this chapter, we present basic elements and the underpinnings for using the notion of participation in the different creative activities in which the users are not only studied as using information objects but also creating them. We present models suggesting how and when to study participants' engagements and involvement in activities that can embed information handling tasks. Finally, a specific framework for studying collaborative activities. This involves some tools and techniques to be considered in studies on collaborative information activities.

CHAPTER 4

# Third Space

In Chapter 2 we explained Third Space as an intersection zone that can be an adaptable and dynamic space where an individual finds or develop new ways of knowing and constructing new world views that differ from prior knowledge and experience (Kuhlthau et al., 2015, p. 32; Kuhlthau and Cole, 2012, p. 1). Third Space can also be the zone or region where participant groups (i.e., stakeholders and end-users) can relate, understand, and combine diverse knowledge and under-standings into new insights and paths for practical activity and thinking to develop information objects (Muller and Druin, 2012). Such a space may have important characteristics and conditions that include aspects such as challenging assumptions, learning reciprocally, and creating new ideas emerging through negotiation and co-creation (Muller and Druin, 2012). Information activities, specifically information sharing, and encountering are very important; these are explored in more detail in the next chapter. We have also noted this in earlier chapters due to its importance. Both the method (participatory design) and the information activities are utilized and involved in what we will present as a space, i.e., Third Space where challenges and problems are overcome, solutions found, and gaps in understanding bridged. We will also note how Third Space relates to a well-es-tablished concept in information behavior, namely "information grounds."

The purpose of this chapter is thus to discuss Third Space as a concept that can be in-terpreted in two different ways, namely: Third Space understood as interpreted in information behavior (which includes literature on guided inquiry and information literacy), and Third Space as interpreted in HCI and participatory design literature. This chapter will conclude by presenting the conditions required for the formation of Third Space as an intersection zone. In Chapter 6, Third Space will be presented as a framework where information activities and interactions (specifically information sharing) occur through the application of participatory design tools and techniques.

## 4.1 THIRD SPACE AS A CONCEPT AND THEORY

Third Space as a concept originally labeled third place first appeared in 1989 in Ray Oldenburg's book, titled: *The Great Good Place*. Oldenburg (1989) describes the *first place* as being one's home, *second place* as the workplace, and *third place* as a public space (i.e., informal meeting places). "The third place is a generic designation for a great variety of public spaces that host the regular, volun-tary, informal, and happily anticipated gatherings of individuals' and is a core setting of informal public life" (Oldenburg, 1989, p. 16). As Oldenburg's (1989) third place concept suggests, these are place-based (concrete, material, generic) spaces with the following characteristics (pp. 20–42):

offers a safe and comfortable neutral ground, move beyond the traditional "escape and relief from stress [of] regular places"; integrates political and social dimensions, particularly the "experiences and relationships afforded"; promotes social equality (i.e., a democratic leveling place); facilitates "conversations [as] the main activity"; highly accessible and proximate to users; nurtures a playful mood; fosters psychological comfort; encourages gatherings by regulars; and supports both the development of new and old friendships. In essence, Oldenburg's (1989) third place can be seen as a democratic, inclusive and permissive space allowing conversations to take place in a playful mode.

Oldenburg (1989) highlights the significance to look at the political and social characteristics of third places which are complemented by Bhabha's (1990) view of the Third Space concept. Bhabha, a post-colonial theorist, "originally used this conceptualization to illustrate how contrasting cultural experiences can combine to create a hybrid transformative space, from which new understandings emerge which are not bound by any one cultural discourse" (McIntyre and Hobson, 2016, p. 138). In essence, Bhabha (1994) views Third Space as an "in-between" space in which identities and literate, social, and cultural practices developed characterized by "hybridity" (also known as hybridity theory). Thus, the development of Third Space from a concept to a theory (Third Space Theory) was inspired by Bhabha in 1994.

The potential of Third Space as a theory was also recognized by Soja (1996). His version of Thirdspace (note different spelling) was largely based on the work of Lefebvre's (1991) spatial trialectics (i.e., three moments of social space) and Foucault's concept of heterotopia; it also resembles Bhabha's (1994) concept of cultural hybridity. Soja (1996) describes the following three spatial notions to explain spatiality.

- **Firstspace:** It is important to recognize the impact of historicality, sociality, and spatiality in understanding social processes in our life-worlds. Here the focus is on analyzing and interpreting the text of physical objects thus forming a perceived space. This is the invisible space surrounding our bodies. A space of complex spatial organization of the social practices that shape our action spaces.

- **Secondspace:** Reality is understood through imagined (envisioned) representation, and spatiality is accounted for as a constitutive (organic, fluid) element of the reality of the world. Therefore, the "imagined" geography is defined in conceived space and becomes the "real" geography. The representations of power and ideology are located in these dominating mental spaces.

- **Thirdspace:** Focuses on making endless sympathetic deconstructions and heuristic reconstructions of perceived space and conceived space by injecting new possibilities into the "lived space." Hence, it draws upon both the material and mental spaces of perceived space and conceived space. A Thirdspace offers spatial thinking in which

*...everything comes together... subjectivity and objectivity, the abstract and concrete, the real and imagined, the knowable and the unimaginable, the repetitive and the differential, structure and agency, mind and body, conscious and the unconscious, the disciplined and the transdisciplinary, everyday life and unending history. Anything which fragments Thirdspace into separate specialized knowledge or exclusive domains—even on the pretext to handling its infinite complexity—destroys its meaning and openness* (pp. 56–57).

Against the latter, a Third Space can be a metaphorical, representational (i.e., Bhabha's [1994] Third Space) or material space (Oldenburg's [1989] third place), within which individuals can make sense of the (sometimes competing) discourses and systems which are prevalent in the other spaces they inhabit.

Various disciplines contributed to shaping current interpretations of Third Space. These include urban environmental design (i.e., tea garden) (Wohl, 2017), linguistic and translation studies (Alfer, 2017), leisure studies (Purnell, 2015), discourse and literacy learning (MacDonald, 2019), tourism landscapes (Amoamo, 2011), HCI (Muller, 2007; Muller and Druin, 2012), and library and information science (Kuhlthau et al., 2015). The importance of studying Third Space in education and information literacy practices (Jónsdóttir et al., 2015; Maniotes, 2005; McDonough, 2014; Skattebol and Arthur, 2014), as well as participatory practices in participatory design (Mitchell and Vaughn, 2011; Muller and Druin, 2012) have also been broadly noted.

The original term of third place has also been noted in work on informal information sharing and information grounds (Pettigrew, 1999; Fisher et al., 2005, 2007; Savolainen, 2009). Information ground is a "synergistic environment(s) temporarily created when people come together for a singular purpose but from whose behavior emerges a social atmosphere that fosters the spontaneous and serendipitous sharing of information" (Pettigrew, 1999, p. 811).

Although input from various disciplines is acknowledged, this chapter will specifically focus on Third Space as understood in information behavior (which includes literature on guided inquiry and information literacy), and Third Space as interpreted in HCI and participatory design literature. We touched on this in Chapter 2 but will now go into more detail.

## 4.2 INFORMATION BEHAVIOR LENS ALIGNED WITH GUIDED INQUIRY AND INFORMATION LITERACY ON THIRD SPACE

Several related terms have been used throughout the information behavior literature to define Third Space, namely: inquiry learning, independent learning, deep learning, dynamic learning space, hybrid space, in-between learning space, safe space, organic space or environment, and learning-centered environment (Kuhlthau et al., 2015). These terms signify that Third Space in the field of information behavior has more of a cognitive annotation as Third Space is used as a learning strategy for engagement and construction of new knowledge (also known as constructivist learning). This learning strategy can be developed through Guided Inquiry Design (GID) which is a research-based framework to develop pedagogical practices for deep learning (Maniotes, 2005). Guided inquiry is based on Kuhlthau's information search process (ISP) which describes thoughts, feelings, and actions in six stages as students construct their own understanding of a topic through the exploration of a variety of information sources (Kuhlthau, 2004). The accessing, analyzing, interpreting, evaluating, gathering, using, and synthesizing of information sources in all forms to promote learning requires students to have information literacy competencies (Kuhlthau et al., 2015).

Against the latter, Third Space viewed from an information behavior lens is aligned with guided inquiry and information literacy as promoted by Kuhlthau et al. (2015). In their work, Third Space creates a flexible model that incorporates constructivist learning through merging a student's personal knowledge system (first space) and curriculum (second space) to produce a guided learning environment. As noted in the preceding section, various disciplines have contributed to the concept of Third Space, however, for this chapter, we will focus on Third Space from an information behavior lens aligned with two central concepts, namely: guided inquiry (constructivist learning) and information literacy.

## 4.2.1   GUIDED INQUIRY

Guided inquiry is based on the philosophy of constructivist learning, the need to create a Third Space for optimal learning, and Kuhlthau's (1991) Information Search Process model (Kuhlthau, 2010). Maniotes (2018, pp. 23–24) highlights that "the basic tenet of guided inquiry is Third Space, a dynamic learning space that connects school learning to the student's world". "It is the 'watermark' of Guided Inquiry, a pervasive underlying impression that influences all aspects of the design and guidance throughout the inquiry process." She furthermore explains that guided inquiry reveals students' holistic experience (i.e., feelings, thoughts and actions) during the process of learning through the seeking of an assortment of information sources (print and electronic sources) (Maniotes, 2018, p. 24). Thus, "guided inquiry is founded on research that reveals students' holistic experience in the process of learning from a variety of sources, described in Kuhlthau's model of the ISP" (Kuhlthau et al., 2015, p. 53).

Guidance in the process of learning can be accomplished through true dialogue and asking real questions to inspire students to learn and construct meaningful methods of sharing what they have learned, also known as guided inquiry learning (Kuhlthau et al., 2015). Furthermore, a zone of intervention, which was molded on Vygotsky's zone of proximal development (1978), can support the construction of new knowledge and gaining of personal understanding during the constructive process of inquiry (Maniotes, 2018). For example, "the zone of intervention is that area in which the student can do with advice and assistance what he or she cannot do alone or can do only with great difficulty" (Kuhlthau, 2004, pp. 128–129). The intervention within this zone enables students to progress in the accomplishment of their tasks. Thus, constructing new knowledge and understanding. Moreover, educators can provide guidance and intervention when they notice students are showing reactions and feelings such as uncertainty or confusion during the information seeking process model to complete a research task. Basically, guided inquiry offers intensive intervention at critical points where instruction, guidance, and reflection are required in the inquiry process to nurture deep personal learning in the Third Space. Thus, "aligning personal interest (outside experience) with curriculum content, developing inquiry questions, working in inquiry circles, and using continuous reflection to develop metacognition" (FitzGerald and Garrison, 2016, p. 667). Students asking real questions can merge their outside experiences with the curriculum. "Real questions are about something genuinely important to students and to which they do not already know the answer" (Kuhlthau et al., 2015, p. 27). Real questions create an organic environment (Third Space) of inquiry in which teachers and students come together because they honestly want to find out and learn. Educators can subtly guide the inquiry through their own questions in this conversation.

Kuhlthau et al. (2015) notes that Third Space interactions promote inspiration, creativity, and curiosity throughout the inquiry process, and lifelong learning once a project is completed. Third Space illustrates the imperative for educationalists to determine when a student requires assistance, and as a result, guidance can be provided to *merge* students' cultural knowledge and personal experience (first space) to better understand their curriculum content (second space), thus creating a dynamic learning and teaching space called the Third Space (Kuhlthau et al., 2015; Maniotes, 2005).

The overlap and merge happen between the first space and second space, also termed *Third Space mergers*, and encourages three types of academic interactions.

- **Intellectual inquiry:** Students want to know more about the text and decide to find answers to their questions from outside sources.

- **Deep reading:** Students closely examine and analyze the text to gain deeper meanings and insight.

- **Social empathy:** Students work from the text to study their relationships with others in the group and display empathy with their colleagues.

Against the latter, it is worth noting that applying these Third Space interactions to deepen learning and meet curriculum goals are directed by three essential characteristics, specifically: *meaningful content* (i.e., creating connections between students' learning journey [curriculum] and their lives); *receptive context* (i.e., learning potential of students and the formative role of educators to mediate thinking, Vygotsky's zone of proximal development); and *variety of modes of expression* (i.e., creative expressions of ideas and information; connected to literacy competencies).

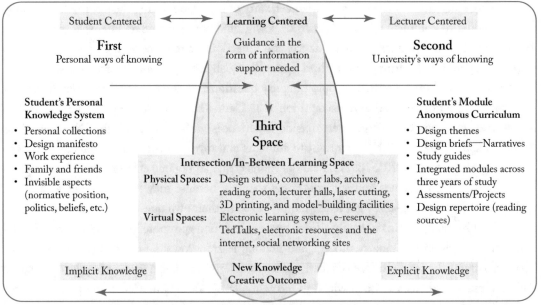

Figure 4.1: Third Space guided inquiry model relevant to architectural design projects in spaces of creativity. Based on Meyer (2016).

For instance, Figure 4.1 was developed from an information behavior study (Meyer, 2016) with architecture students doing architectural design projects in spaces of creativity. The findings of the study suggested that the Third Space concept can bridge the gap between architecture students' theoretical knowledge (curriculum knowledge) and practical application (personal knowledge) to generate creative outcomes. It also provided insights for lecturers regarding how curriculum-based projects or tests can be constructed to support students' personal knowledge in complex learning environments. Furthermore, the Third Space concept in correlation with guided inquiry promoted collective idea generation and sharing during architectural design projects in spaces of creativity. Thus, supporting information activities (e.g., information needs, seeking, searching, sharing, selecting, extracting, encountering, browsing, visualization) relevant to the design projects, as well as providing information and information support needed during architectural design projects. Guidance by means of providing information and information support included acting as a creative springboard, assistance to access information, virtual (Online InterStudio and IntraStudio information sites and databases) assistance by generating a creative student hub, and availability of past and present design projects.

## 4.2.2   INFORMATION LITERACY

Harmansah and Shepherd (2012) explain that Third Space refers to the boundary zone in which two cultures meet, hybrid identities take shape, new discourses develop, and various forms of literacy are created. These forms of literacy have been mentioned in the work by Meyer et al. (2018), namely: socio-critical literacy (Gutiérrez, 2008), visual literacy (Lee, 2009), content literacy (Moje et al., 2004), literacy learning (Cook, 2005; Pane, 2007), digital literacy (Potter and McDougall, 2017), and information literacy (Kuhlthau, 2010; Kuhlthau et al., 2015; Verbaan and Cox, 2014).

A limited amount of Third Space literature focusing on information literacy is available (Elmborg, 2011; Elmborg et al., 2015; Kuhlthau, 2010; Kuhlthau et al., 2015; Verbaan and Cox, 2014). The predominant focus of this literature is the use of the Third Space concept for the provision of information literacy skills through inquiry in diverse learning, living, and working situations. Kuhlthau (2010, p. 22) highlights information literacy as one of the five types of learning achieved through guided inquiry. The other types of learning include "learning how to learn, curriculum content, literacy competence and social skills." In the inquiry process, "students learn the underlying concepts of locating, evaluating and using information that is transferable to a wide range of situations of information seeking and use," therefore learning information literacy skills (Kuhlthau, 2010, p. 23). Thus, the inquiry process offers the opportunity to produce a Third Space. Guided inquiry empowers students to create their own connections within the inquiry process that inspires the development of information literacy skills, and builds expertise and ownership (Kuhlthau, 2010, p. 21).

Against the later, developing information literacy skills through inquiry in the Third Space encourage students to:

- use the information to find meaning and to gain a deeper understanding during learning;

- organize information to provide access to ideas, facts, and multiple perspectives;

- perform various types of information searching such as preliminary, exploratory and comprehensive (here students can practice differentiating, chaining, and extracting for information deep learning), and summary searching;

- evaluate sources of information to select the most useful and valuable information to stimulate enlightenment, reflection, and curiosity;

- decide and choose information in diverse formats, nurtures multiple ways of learning and thinking; and

- share information, knowledge and expertise to promote collaboration, support creative problem solving, reinforce learning, and help others to learn (Kuhlthau et al., 2015).

## 4.3    HUMAN–COMPUTER INTERACTION AND PARTICIPATORY DESIGN PERSPECTIVE ON THIRD SPACE

There have been several calls within the field of HCI for reciprocal or mutual learning in hybrid spaces (Muller, 2007). For instance, Maher et al. (2006) discussed the formation of virtual design spaces for sharing various perspectives, expertise, and knowledge. Additionally, Fanderclai (1996) and Tscheligi et al. (1995) accentuated that these hybrid virtual spaces could produce new dynamics, understandings, communications, relationships, and new methods of learning. Furthermore, Merkel et al. (2004, pp. 7–8) noted the need for "a new set of skills and competencies that go beyond technical design skills…to create conditions that encourage a collaborative design process and active reflection…for working with groups…that push on the traditional boundaries between users and designers." Lastly, Thackara (2000) stresses that the concept of Third Space offers the desired hybridity to HCI studies.

Within HCI, the concept of a Third Space occurs in "the border or boundary region between two domains, or two spaces," thus frequently creating a region of overlap or hybridity (Muller, 2007, p. 1064). For instance, the creation of a third (hybrid) space between software professionals and end-users which encompasses "an unpredictable and changing combination of attributes of each of the two bordering spaces" (Muller, 2007, p. 1064), enhancing knowledge exchange. This hybrid space develops from the difficulties and variances in knowledge and experience levels (i.e., *tensions*) of the participating individuals. Thus, participants in a learning or other creative situation can combine knowledge to co-construct new meanings, concepts and alliances. Muller and Druin (2012, p. 2) define a set of attributes of Third Space experiences, such as challenging assumptions, learning reciprocally, and creating new ideas, co-creation of identities, understandings, relationships, and polyvocal (many-voiced) dialogue across and through differences.

Suchman (2002), for example, highlights the need for dialogue across boundaries between the fractional perspectives of developers and end-users within the field of HCI. Moreover, Fowles (2000) talks about converting the "symmetry of ignorance" (mutual lack of understanding among designers and users) into a corresponding "symmetry of knowledge" through symmetries of learning and symmetries of participation. Correspondingly, Holmström (1995) investigated a "gap in rationalities" between developers/designers and users. As a result, "creating regions of overlap where multiple perspectives can come into mutual knowledge and, potentially, alliance—with the creation of the hybrid spaces in which objectivity can emerge through constructive and creative discussion, understanding, dialogue, negotiation, and mutual learning" (Muller, 2007, p. 1064).

In essence, the use of a Third Space within HCI has resulted in the advancement of valuable methods, tools, and techniques to develop and foster active participation, mutual learning, communication, group collaboration, negotiation of assumptions, innovation, and critical thinking and reflection in design, based on merging perspectives across disciplines. This can be seen in Figure 6.3. Participatory theories, practices, and methods, such as participatory design, might lend itself toward mutual validation of diverse perspectives to construct solutions to complex human problems or to create new relationships, knowledge and understanding of our workplace practices, and everyday situations and technologies.

Participatory design involves future uses in a design process, giving them a voice, and empowering them to influence the design of their own future tools, technologies, services, and work practices and procedures. It brings different stakeholders together to collectively share their experiences, negotiate requirements and actively contribute to the common goal of the design (Simonsen and Robertson, 2012). In order to facilitate the possibility for individuals to cooperate and collaborate (Hansen et al., 2016), tools or methods to overcome social, cultural, professional, and communication barriers in teams with mixed expertise need to be recognized. The involvement of the users generally had a social notion and tried to nurture the democratization of the workplace. A number of researchers (Muller, 2007; Muller and Druin, 2012; Schuck et al., 2017) have mentioned that participatory design methods create a Third Space characterized as boundary-crossing, hybrid, fluid, and transformative.

Third Space in HCI promotes a multidisciplinary nature of participation. Thus, including stakeholders and end-users from different domains to participate in participatory design projects (Muller and Druin, 2012). This can form a region of changing combinations of ideas, attributes, and assumptions of each of the two bordering spaces (also known as border or boundary regions) where enhanced knowledge exchange, mutual learning, and collaboration is possible within this space (Muller and Druin, 2012).

Overall, participatory design and the Third Space share the following common characteristics: learning reciprocally (mutual learning), collaboration, trust, challenging of assumptions, creation of new ideas through negotiation, and co-creation of identities, relationships, and understandings, values, empowerment, and sharing polyvocal (many-voiced) dialogues through and across differences (Muller, 2007).

## 4.4    CONDITIONS REQUIRED FOR THIRD SPACE AS AN INTERSECTION ZONE

A Third Space is a dynamic, diverging, and converging and moving space affected by different conditions in time and space as well as the participation of collaborators (Wang, 2007, p. 389). Third Spaces are characterized as being fluid, porous spaces, thus not bounded or closed, moving participants between and across public, private, and work-related spheres (Punie, 2007). Furthermore, these spaces are also characterized as being transformative, and this hybridity is conceptualized in terms of the borderline conditions (crossing over or border regions) that exist there (Bhabha, 1994). This is a vital feature, labeled as a border intellectual, in the work of Paulo Freire (Giroux, 2006). Crossing borders can be both literally and metaphorically. Thus, border crossing is usually associated with complexities experienced by individuals co-existing in a world with shifting social, cultural, and political conditions. In addition, this acknowledgment of complexities intrinsic to crossing boundaries (in a Third Space) is a valuable technique to think about the forms of interactions (with information objects) and types of new knowledge constructed, e.g., new information objects.

Focusing on the Third Space in the field of information behavior and HCI, there are specific characteristics unique to each of these disciplines, as illustrated in Table 4.1.

Table 4.1: Third Space in information behavior and HCI—based on selected literature cited in the preceding section

|  | Information Behavior Third Space | HCI Third Space |
|---|---|---|
| Known by various terms | Intersection zone, in-between learning space. | Boundary region, hybrid space. |
| Facilitation space | Facilitate information literacy guidance (mediation) in the form of guided inquiry. | Produce high and low prototyping (such as paper/clay or digital prototypes). |
| Experiences and knowledge development space | Intersect personal experiences (first space) with curricula (second space), even involving people from different disciplines. | Represent a shift in knowledge and experience. Understand the relationships between different levels of experience. |
| Supportive space | Safe space for zones of intervention at decision points (question-asking). | Negotiation space. |
| Learning space | Constructivist learning. | Mutual learning (social learning). |
| Collaborative space | Collaboration and co-construction of knowledge are focused on learning objectives and learning outcomes. | Purposeful collaboration, immediate (specific objective), and often inquiry-driven; creative co-construction of new knowledge commons. |
| Creative and creation space | Innovation-driven: Support the generation of new ideas, knowledge, and insights. | Goal-driven design: Produce objects, tools, systems, practices, and services. |
| Shared outcome space | Working toward a common vision/purpose. | Working for the common good (symbiotic). |

From the characteristics identified for Third Spaces in information behavior and HCI, there are additional conditions noted throughout the literature significant to the formation of physical, virtual, and mental Third Spaces. See Tables 4.2 and 4.3 to see these conditions.

| Table 4.2: Conditions required for a physical Third Space | |
| --- | --- |
| **Authors** | **Conditions Required for a Physical Third Space** |
| Oldenburg (1989) | Eight characteristics for a physical third place:<br>• **Neutral (political) ground:** Welcomes individuals from all walks of life (i.e., different opinions and life views). No financial, political, or legal ties and invitations are needed.<br>• **Leveling place:** No prerequisites for participation in terms of economic and social status or hierarchy.<br>• **Focus on conversation:** Main activity is face-to-face conversation which is stimulating and engaging with a good-natured tone.<br>• **Accessible and accommodating:** Easily accessible both socially and geographically.<br>• **Have regulars:** Regulars welcome newcomers and shape the "tone" of a place.<br>• **Keep a low profile:** It is physical characteristics and design avoids pretentiousness. They are comfortable, frugal, and relaxing.<br>• **Playful atmosphere:** A playful, loud, and conversation-filled atmosphere is allowed and encouraged.<br>• **Home away from home (welcoming and belonging):** It should promote a safe and steady feeling. Thus, producing a sense of ownership or that a piece of yourself is firmly fixed in your place. |
| Various literature in Calderon (2016) | Three aspects of communities in third places:<br>• **Aspects of "place":** Central to human experiences, particularly in society. It introduces the notions of location (i.e., physical setting), ensemble (i.e., group of characteristics and human activities within space), and insideness (i.e., sense of sharing). Thus, defining and classifying the various places of our lives.<br>• **Aspects of "Third Place":** Categorize characteristics of Third Places through the concepts of governance (high/low neutrality and high/low inclusiveness), location and appearance, and playful ambiance.<br>• **Aspects of "social capital":** Considers an approach to understanding community performance by adding value to social interactions and social links. Also discusses the differences in types of social connections (e.g., bridging or bonding) types of social capital (trust and reciprocity, mutual obligations), and types of capital reach and collective gain. |

| Calderon (2016) | Third Space dimensions:<br>• **Sociality dimension** (social capital type of reciprocity) gathers aspects of interpersonal socialization through the concept of social capital, particularly reciprocity, density, and centrality.<br>• **Publicity dimension** (ownership) gathers aspects of governance, particularly information ownership, accessibility, and privacy.<br>• **Physicality dimension** (all Third Place aspects) gathers aspects that relate to physical aspects of technology and places. |
|---|---|

| Table 4.3: Conditions required for a virtual Third Space | |
|---|---|
| **Authors** | **Conditions Required for a Virtual Third Space** |
| Wright (2012) | Adaption of Oldenburg's (1989) eight characteristics of physical third places to include virtual Third Spaces: <br> • **Structural characteristics:** <br>   · *Place:* Physical and virtual; geographic proximity is not a necessary condition for a community to form. <br>   · *Commerce:* Must be free from both government and commercial control but this is debatable. <br>   · *Neutrality:* Political decision-making and the extent to which political discourse becomes polarized–political function (power dynamics). <br>   · *Inclusivity and access:* Eliminate the digital divide and support anonymity. <br>   · *Low profile:* Facilitate equality. <br> • **Participatory characteristics:** <br>   · *The regulars:* Welcome newcomers and set the tone of the space. <br>   · *Communication and mood:* Humor crucial to facilitate political talk; lack of social/physical cues. <br>   · *Rationale for participation:* Must be a mutual/pecuniary beneficiary and have personal gain. |
| Waterhouse, McLaughlin, McLellan, and Morgan (2009) | Three main conditions required for real and imagined Third Spaces: <br> • **Cultural conditions and historical narratives:** Multi-voices to minority group people and acknowledgment of the hybridity of cultures in defiance of ethnocentric traditions. <br> • **Borderline conditions (hybrid and transformative) also known as border intellectualism:** Crossing of borders both literally and metaphorically in which maps of knowledge, social relations, and values are increasingly being negotiated and re-written. The boundary region is fluid, flexible, creative, multilayered, and multidimensional. <br> • **Structural conditions:** Requires physical location to explore issues of emancipation, dominance, and power (locus of control), which are inherent in the dynamics and discourse of collaboration. Requires metaphysical location for critical engagement. |
| Kosari and Amoori (2018) | Components and triggers needed for the formation of a blended synthetic Third Space: <br> • Identity, integration, and imagination are the three basic components needed for the formation of a blended synthetic Third Space (blended mental spaces). <br> • Communication that triggers dynamic creative processes that connect the first space (real space) and the second space (virtual space) to form the Third Space (blended mental space). |

Against the later, conditions required for the formation of Third Spaces to support participatory activities (i.e., participatory design as a method) include focusing on the structure (physical, virtual, or mental), social capital and connections, cultural diversity and equality, power dynamics (political talk), hybridity and transformation (borderline/boundaries), participation (including communication methods and tools); publicity (ownership, privacy, and accessibility); tools and material to facilitate ideas and visions; commence (personal gains); ethics; triggers of activation (i.e., creativity, playful atmosphere); and invisible factors (emotions, social cues, facial expressions, body language, and trust). For each of these conditions, there is considerable scope for further research, specifically in relation to participatory design projects.

## 4.5    SUMMARY

In this chapter, we discussed the concept of Third Space from two interpretations, namely: Third Space related to information behavior and HCI which included participatory design. We also introduced various conditions required for this intersection zone to occur in Third Space (see Tables 4.2 and 4.3). Third Space in the field of HCI provides a boundary region (or intersection zone) where individuals can interact over time, across devices (space and contexts), and with individuals from diverse knowledge domains. The importance of guided inquiry and information literacy in Third Space information behavior literature has been noted. Furthermore, several information-related activities have been noted in the information behavior literature related to Third Spaces such as information seeking, searching, selecting, using, sharing, encountering, and question asking (Maniotes, 2005; Meyer, 2016; Meyer et al., 2018, 2020). The next chapter will delve deeper into the concepts of information sharing, information encountering, and other information interaction activities to study them through various lenses such as information behavior and information practice.

CHAPTER 5

# Information Sharing and Other Information Activities

In participatory design projects, different types of information are shared in diverse formats. Facts, ideas, values, coordination information on the processes of participatory design, and even emotional experiences are shared verbally, through emails, documents, process charts, artifacts, mind maps, information-rich drawings, pictures, audio and video recordings (Bao and Bouthillier, 2007; Cochran et al., 2008; Ginige et al., 2014; Longo, 2014; McDonnell, 2009; Skeels, 2010; Talja, 2002), and also physical activities that people are doing together. This chapter will synthesize findings on the nature of information sharing in participatory design, the type of information shared, tools involved and output created, dynamics experienced, intervening variables and challenges, and the in-tandem manifestation with other information activities. We will search for literature of how a Third Space is acknowledged in research on participatory design and information activities to inform our argument for an appropriate TSIB study framework to guide research on information activities related to the evolvement of knowledge and worldviews of a diversity of participants and stakeholders working towards the fulfillment of the purpose and goals of participatory design projects in diverse contexts. This chapter will focus on information sharing. We will show how appropriate research lenses and theories can deepen understanding.

## 5.1 INTRICACY AND CONTEXTUALIZATION OF INFORMATION SHARING

In a society looking to address contemporary challenges and social outcomes, the scope of participatory design could be extended to a diversity of contexts involving people from different cultures, customs, and language groups. It should then be worth expanding our perceptions of the various forms information may take in such different contexts, the formats in which information might be shared, and the cultural values people may hold for information sharing. Language and the meaning of words and interpretations shared between people then also becomes even more important. Grenersen et al. (2016), for example, explain in a study with Sami people in the arctic region how the landscape can convey information and how the rich Sámi snow terminology distinguishes many hundreds of terms for snow. Language and interpretation have been shown to be very important in cross-cultural participatory design, working with Indigenous communities and especially for sharing information and knowledge in such contexts and participatory design projects (Conley Tyler et al., 2008).

Foster (2007) used visual art, poetry, and short-film making as emotive methods of collecting data and drama as a means to share (i.e., to disseminate) the results—thus different types of information and means of information sharing. Apart from all sharing information, these methods all require interaction with information and practical ability.

Information sharing and interactions between people involve complex cognitive activities such as analytical reasoning, problem-solving and sense-making, that may be performed through the use of interactive participatory design tools such as visual analytics, decision support, and communication, planning, and educational tools. "Through interaction with visual representations of information at the visual interface of these tools, a joint, coordinated cognitive system is formed" (Parsons and Sedig, 2014). Jones et al. (2018) identified various issues that can have an influence on activities, namely: (a) context; (b) activity (usual and contingent); and (c) influence with activities such as information processing, source-user interaction, information evaluation, selection of information, information use, clinical reasoning, and clinical decisions. Information sharing is one of many activities and should in particular focus on democratic participation and building agency between participants and working towards shared meaning and understanding. There are many other activities such as information structuring, information de-structuring, information searching, information organization, and information management. Information sharing happens in all phases of a project from the initiation of the project, the definition of the purpose and goals and the renegotiation of the shared purpose and goals once all participants are on board, throughout data collection and the development and testing of prototypes up to the evaluation of the success of the project. Information sharing manifests in all steps and tasks such as building relationships, selecting and inviting participants, starting interactions, and defining roles. It also happens during documenting ideas and decisions, interacting with and involving participants, facilitating access to information and information sharing inside as well as outside the participatory design project, following up and continuation of interactions (Korošak et al., 2018; Roschelle et al., 2006; Zaphiris and Constantinou, 2007). When people collaborate on projects, the nature, type, and intensity of information being shared differ across phases and stages (Ellis, 1989). (Collaborative information behavior is explained in Section 2.1.) The nature of tasks and roles influences information seeking and information sharing (Tao and Tombros, 2017; Vakkari, 1999).

Context is important in participatory design. Some projects are highly sophisticated and rely on the state-of-the-art technology and highly qualified, interdisciplinary experts (Clack et al., 2019). Others are in communities with poorly developed information infrastructures and vast differences between stakeholders' educational levels and cultural backgrounds (Abbass-Dick et al., 2018).

What they have in common is that participatory design requires a space that is open to reflection, negotiation, and the democratic evolving of new ideas, innovations, experiences, knowledge, skills, learning, meaning-making, and shared meaning and above all, the ability and the task to create a future object, service, or behavior. This space, Third Space, has been extensively discussed in Chapter 4. Benyon (2014) also offers valuable input on interaction spaces. Information sharing can be done verbally pre and during participatory (design) projects that involves creating an object, system or service. It is an essential activity in this Third Space where participants cognitively process and internalize information in all its possible forms to make decisions and to develop solutions and new products (Ginige et al., 2014; Keshavarz, 2008; Longo, 2014; Skeels, 2010). Both information sharing and information processing manifest at different points in time and through different means. The same would apply to other information activities such as information interaction.

Information sharing happens in tandem and in a symbiotic relationship with many other information interaction activities such as information seeking, collaborative information seeking, information retrieval and information encountering, as well as information deconstruction, reconstruction, assembling, and concept adjustment as well as cognitive activities such as information processing and sense-making (Bessant, 2009; Fang and Strobel, 2011; Hertzum and Hansen, 2019; Jiang et al., 2019; Keshavarz, 2008; Shah, 2012; Somerville and Howard, 2010). Despite the use of information activities in participatory design projects and the importance of information sharing in participatory design, relatively few studies have, however, reported on information behavior and information practices in participatory design (exceptions being Keshavarz, 2008; Meyer et al., 2018; Muller and Druin, 2012; Nickpour et al., 2014). Van der Velden and Mörtberg (2015) explain how "reflection-in-action" during the design process is used to cultivate critical discussions among various stakeholders. Power imbalances also need to be addressed (McIntyre-Mills, 2010) to reveal active knowledge and understanding (Lee et al., 2017).

For successful participatory design, the growth and evolvement of all stakeholders in a Third Space influenced by information sharing and other information interaction activities need to move beyond individual knowledge and views to new knowledge that can result in new products that fulfill the purpose of the participatory design project must be understood. These activities may be storytelling, drawing, and communicating through other physical or digital objects (Eriksson and Hansen, 2017) such as the use of storyboards and video clips. Information behavior and information practice, and specifically collaborative information behavior (cf., Section 2.1) and practice, supplemented by applicable theories (Fisher et al., 2006), are appropriate research lenses that can be applied. However, as we will show, an appropriate Third Space framework is needed to explore the scope and depth of information sharing and other information interaction activities and their symbiotic connection with cognitive processing, internalization and transformation (Wipawayang-kool and Teng, 2016). A participatory design approach and a Third Space can also guide information behavior research, focusing on a Third Space as a place to study information behavior research supported by participatory design.

Participatory design is marked by collaboratively striving for clarity of coherent visions, goals, and needs (Simonsen and Hertzum, 2012) in a democratic manner involving all stakeholders and resulting in the application of new shared knowledge in decision making and the development of something new, e.g., a new product or information object (Keshavarz, 2008). The knowledge base of the participatory design team depends on the willingness to share information (Salter and Schulz, 2005). This is especially important when it comes to sharing information on prior errors and failures (Salter et al., 2008). (Information sharing is a condition for both participatory design and Third Space.)

How people are enabled to share information in a democratic manner, how they engage in a culture of openness, how they experience the right to give their inputs and the dynamics between stakeholders are important (Mor and Winters, 2008). We should not

> *...take users [participants or stakeholders] only as information sources or objects for design, but it is also important for users to participate in the design process at informative, consultative or participative levels, as democratic participation and skill enhancement are important concerns* (Keshavarz, 2008, p. 396).

Through different levels of involvement, participants share information with the main purpose to achieve their individual as well as common interests in a project (Bao and Bouthillier, 2007, p. 1).

Participants explicitly or implicitly share different types of information and there are different levels of involvement during a participatory design project or workshop. They do so from their expertise, tacit knowledge, lived experiences, and search heuristics (McDonnell, 2009; Somerville and Howard, 2010; Zhao et al., 2019) as well as their thoughts on others' thinking, ideas, and negotiation of positions. They share such information purposefully or unintentionally; they might deliberately share information to stimulate creative design ideas, or they might restrain from sharing information.

Participants share (prior) knowledge and experiences *relevant* as well as *peripheral* during a participatory design project utilizing one or more participatory design workshops (cf., Chapter 3). They share information from *inside* the project and information from *outside* the project. They obtain new information when needed from outside the project by searching for information resources such as books, articles, research reports and grey literature or Internet information resources. They also obtain information through their personal connections, social and community networks; they draw on their social capital and professional work experiences. Participants can actively and purposefully seek information (to share) due to a gap in their knowledge or a gap in the knowledge of the design team or they can share information they accidentally encountered (Makri and Warwick, 2010). They can seek information individually or collaboratively (Hansen and Järvelin, 2005; Shah and Marchionini, 2010). They can capture information (Shenton, 2010).

There are differences in the urgency for information and the levels of uncertainty experienced by stakeholders (Uitdewilligen and Waller, 2018). Even in conventional information-seeking people's perceptions of uncertainty, complexity, construction, and sources in information tasks differ and change during the information seeking process (Kuhlthau, 1999). Zaphiris and Constantinou (2007) noted participant member fatigue.

Information sharing can occur concurrently with other information activities such as information seeking, information retrieval, and information encountering. The term information sharing is often used interchangeably with information exchange, information transfer, information giving, and information distribution (Janiūnienė and Macevičiūtė, 2016; Talja and Hansen, 2006; Widén and Hansen, 2012; Wilson, 2010a, b). It might not be possible to clearly demarcate each of these. Most importantly for participatory design is the connection between reflection, information and cognitive processing, and information sharing and how new meaning and new knowledge and new objects are constructed resulting in collaborative decision-making and new products. Participatory design specifically depends on many things like collaboration, joint motivation, willingness to share, understanding of a specific problem, and the willingness to change a specific behavior. The scope and depth of understanding of information sharing and the interaction with other information interaction activities and especially related activities such as mentioned in Figure 5.1 are very important. Such findings would take place in Third Space following the discussion and arguments presented in Chapter 4.

## 5.2    APPROPRIATE RESEARCH LENSES

Many researchers have called for the need to take findings on information behavior and information practice into account for the practical design of information systems and information services (Agarwal, 2018; Fidel and Pejtersen, 2004; Hepworth et al., 2014). This could apply to (i) systems and services supported by different design approaches such as participatory design, and (ii) tools and interventions supporting information sharing and information interaction in a participatory Third Space. In a study on information behavior and participatory design, Keshavarz (2008) notes the importance of understanding users' information activities (i.e., information needs, information seeking, information searching and information retrieval), as well as context-based aspects such as tasks, environment, and organizational setting during the participatory design of information retrieval systems.

A research lens determines what a researcher will observe and detect; it impacts findings and decisions. Many examples can be noted (Bukhari et al., 2016; Case and Given, 2016; Ford, 2015; Wilson, 1997). A research lens allows researchers to report on the components, processes, and experiences, and the influence of intervening variables such as diverse educational, professional, interdisciplinary or multidisciplinary, and cultural backgrounds, diverse experiences, skills, expertise, personalities and learning styles (Heinström, 2006; Scandurra et al., 2008), tasks and roles (Leckie et al., 1996), and the influence of prior experience (Johnson and Case, 2012). A research lens also allows researchers to observe movement, evolvement, and changes in cognitive and affective experiences, thoughts and feelings (Kuhlthau, 1991), the importance of context including the environment, the person in context, the changes in information behavior between project phases and stages (Ellis, 1989), preferences for information sources, and the nonlinear nature of information seeking (Foster, 2004). In participatory design, the diversity of participants, the definition of purpose and goals in a collaborative and democratic manner, nature of phases, the need for creativity and new products, the prominence of information sharing, and the importance of trust, acceptance, and respect in information sharing require more from a framework to guide studies on participatory design per se (Meyer et al., 2020). Models, frameworks, and theories can serve as research lenses. A framework by Hansen and Widén (2017) explores the embeddedness of collaborative information seeking in information culture where both environmental (cultural), as well as collaborative aspects of organizational information behavior and the emphasis on awareness, might shed additional light on how information is used in collaborative settings. Models on information sharing per se that might also be noted include Du (2014), Erdelez and Rioux (2000), Luo et al. (2020), Panahi et al. (2016), Pilerot (2012), Savolainen (2017), Tabak and Willson (2012) and as implied in the work of Shah (2012, 2017). Some models instead of information sharing, refer to "information transfer" and "information exchange" (McKenzie, 2003; Wilson, 1999, 2010a, 2010b) while others focus more on communication (Robson and Robinson, 2013, 2015). An excellent review of information sharing models is offered by Savolainen (2019).

This framework and a nascent framework by Meyer et al. (2020), could guide the development of a TSIB study framework for participatory design where information behavior and information sharing are studied in participatory design. That can also be used for a TSIB framework where information behavior research applies participatory design methodology and processes. That is what we intend to argue for in Chapter 6 (cf., Figures 6.1a,b).

The need for sense-making (Solomon, 1997a,b) and filling gaps in knowledge is seldom explicitly acknowledged in information behavior models, exceptions being the work by Brenda Dervin (1993) and Natalja Godbold (2006, 2013). Information sharing cannot be separated from information needs and anomalies in knowledge (ASK) (Belkin, 1980; Cole, 2012). There are also many challenges in recognizing and articulating information needs (Shenton, 2007; Taylor, 1968). More research from the perspective of collaborative information behavior is therefore needed to enlighten work on participatory design and the collaborative recognition of information needs.

There are different phases of construction of knowledge (e.g., Kuhlthau, 1988) and different levels of awareness of information needs and abilities to clearly express such information needs (Taylor, 1968). Work by Wilson (1981) and Shenton (2007) in particular focus on challenges with dormant information needs that are not recognized. In participatory design, each challenge can have multiple outcomes, and endeavors to resolve challenges often construct new, possibly even more complex, challenges (Rittel, 1972), which might trigger new information needs. How information needs manifest in the context of creativity is also important.

Collaborative information behavior can also be useful as a research lens to study information sharing in participatory design projects (Blake and Pratt, 2006a, b; Hyldegård, 2006; Karunakaran et al., 2013; Reddy and Jansen, 2008). These models emphasize single, simple, and direct information interactions for individuals and complex, multiple, and conversational information interactions when people collaborate (Karunakaran et al., 2013). People can also collaborate when they retrieve, extract, verify, and analyze information; they need to synthesize information. The discovery of new things could be collaborative rather than individual. Synthesis and decisions on the salience of information are very important (Blake and Pratt, 2006a, b). They suggest the addition of a synthesis stage between the collection of information and presentation. Hyldegård (2006) found that emotional and cognitive experiences do not only result from information seeking activities but also from work task activities and intragroup interactions. At the end of a project some members of a collaborating group still felt uncertain, frustrated, and disappointed, which partly was associated with a mismatch in motivations, ambitions, and project focus among group members.

Complex problems lead to the need for significant communication and direct interactions with several people and systems. There may be direct interaction to address fact-finding and conversational interaction to address exploratory search, problem resolving, and decision making (Reddy and Jansen, 2008).

Another lens is information practice (Savolainen, 2007, p. 109). Information practice emphasizes constructivism: "The discourse on information behavior primarily draws on the cognitive viewpoint, while information practice is mainly inspired by the ideas of social constructionism." It relates to situated action and communities of practices that can reveal how people learn and share information and also negotiate meanings, values, and objectives in collaborative settings such as workplaces and information use as discursive action (Savolainen, 2007). Communities of practice stem from the work of Lave and Wenger (Wenger, 1998). The concept of information practice is also elaborated by Talja and Hansen (2006) who argue that information practices are firmly embedded in work and other social practices and that these practices draw on the social practice of a community of practitioners, a sociotechnical infrastructure, and a common language. Such a language can, however, not be taken for granted in participatory design; challenges with language and meaning, especially in cross-cultural work, were also noted at the start of this chapter.

For Savolainen (2007, p. 126), the concepts of behavior and practice "seem to denote the same phenomena: they deal with the ways in which people do things." Although the concepts both refer to the ways in which people deal with information, the difference is

> *… that within the discourse on information behavior, the "dealing with information" is primarily seen to be triggered by needs and motives, while the discourse on information practice accentuates the continuity and habitualization of activities affected and shaped by social and cultural factors.*

Talja and McKenzie (2007, p. 100) emphasize how information practice relates to discursive approaches to information in context:

> *Discursive information studies capture the socially and culturally shaped practices of creating, using, seeking, accessing, and sharing information. The change in terminology, the preference of the concept "information practice" over "information behavior," conveys a view that information needs, seeking, and use are constituted socially and dialogically since all human practices are social.*

From their perspective "discursive approaches to information practices view information needs, seeking, and use as part of or as embedded in cultural, social, or organizational practice and question the validity of models that 'de-domain' information practices" (Talja and McKenzie, 2007, p. 100). The community of practice in which information is generated, shared, and negotiated is important and "a deeper understanding of how groups organize their work practices through interacting with texts, coworkers, technologies, and other objects of the material world" (Talja and McKenzie, 2007, p. 100) is essential.

Applying an information practice lens, Dunne (2002) could note changes in progressive situations. Progression also featured in the information practice work of McKenzie (2003, 2004). Somerville (2013) could reveal evolving, change, discovery, and exploration. Change in information behavior across different daily life situations is not uncommon (Julien and Michels, 2004) and could in particular be expected in participatory design and constructivist contexts. Considering the complexity of participatory design and collaborative information behavior an appropriate research lens should allow us to study such change and progression and the impact on information sharing and other information interaction activities. As can be seen from Figure 5.1, there are many activities in addition to information sharing taking place in a Third Space. We are noting only a few types: information activities that will include information sharing and information encountering, learning activities, cognition activities, reflective activities, participative activities, positioning activities, creative activities, and emotional activities. Figure 5.1 also shows two boundary objects.

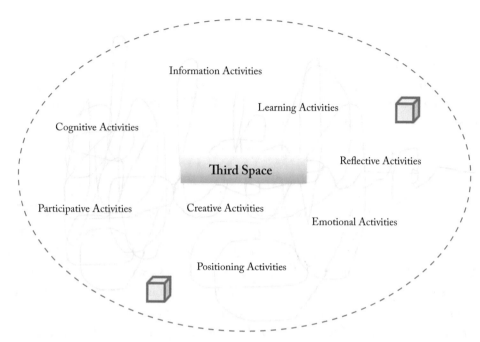

Figure 5.1: Typical participant activities taking place in Third Space.

Sometimes additional research lenses are needed in participatory design such as: cognitive views; cultural-historical activity theory; feminist views and theories such as feminist phronetic theory; indigenous ethnography; information poverty theory; sociology of knowledge; Latour's actor-network theory; learning theory; power and empowerment theories; social theory and social science theory; and theories of social constructivism (DiSalvo et al., 2017; Duckles and Moses, 2018; Faiola, 2007; Foster, 2007; Godjo et al., 2015; Spinuzzi, 2005; Yeh, 2007; Zaphiris and Constantinou, 2007; Zemits et al., 2015). These lenses are useful to understand power relations, constructing new meaning and knowledge, and many other dynamics in a participatory design Third Space. Lenses for constructivist learning and ways of knowing on a professional, personal, and epistemological level, and to bridge gaps in the learning of participants from different backgrounds are especially important (Zanotti and Palomino-Schalscha, 2016). In addition, sense-making as presented in the work of Dervin and Foreman-Wernet (2003) might also be a useful lens.

A TSIB study framework presents as a spatial and temporal context where new knowledge, understanding, and creativity manifest through information sharing and other information interaction activities, collective utilization of informational resources and artifacts, and through collective information and cognitive processing (Mesmer-Magnus and DeChurch, 2009). Progression in context and a variety of intervening variables other than what is normally noted in information behavior and information practice studies are at play. An appropriate research lens that might be information behavior, information practice, or collaborative information behavior or elements of these, supplemented by appropriate theories is needed to allow researchers to observe these phenomena per se in a Third Space as a facilitating space in participatory design. Without an appropriate lens, much might go unnoticed. This would also apply when using participatory design as a methodology for information behavior studies. A critical interpretive synthesis (Corrado et al., 2020) is thus needed to identify appropriate theories.

## 5.3    FINDINGS ON INFORMATION SHARING IN PARTICIPATORY DESIGN AND RELATED CONTEXTS

Following the introductory part of this chapter and the section on the intricacy and contextualization of information sharing (cf., Section 5.1) the following subsections will report on findings on how information is shared in participatory design, the tools, the dynamics, and the intervening variables (i.e., enablers and challenges). There is limited literature available on information sharing specifically related to participatory design. We therefore also considered findings on co-design, bonded design, collaborative information sharing, and joint/team decision making (Zha et al., 2019). We considered findings from a diversity of participatory design contexts and purposes ranging from new products (Abbass-Dick et al., 2018) to new styles of organizational communication and shared leadership (Somerville and Howard, 2010), and farms in remote rural areas (Byrne and Sahay, 2007; Schaap et al., 2013).

### 5.3.1    HOW INFORMATION IS SHARED

Information can be shared from inside and outside participatory design contexts—spontaneously or purposefully, e.g., for collective reflection and understanding or to stimulate creativity (Byrne and Sahay, 2007). Information can be shared both verbally and visually (Barcellini et al., 2015) or through tactile probes (Ginige et al., 2014; Longo, 2014; Skeels, 2010) in face-to-face interactions using "brown bag" lunches, virtual meetings, or wiki-based intranets (Somerville and Howard, 2010). Often, hybrid approaches allowing for combinations of tools and means of interaction are used.

A variety of tools are available to share and collect information in participatory activities. These should be appropriate to the participant composition, complexity, and nature of the context, and should support both the processes of participatory design and the purposes of information sharing. Tools should support both individual and collective reflection, different socio-cognitive experiences, tasks, and domains, deepening participants' understanding, and reaching the purpose and goal of a project to "produce a design with an aim of creating an emotional investment for the users" (Parviainen et al., 2017, p. 1). Widely used techniques and tools include workshops, collage, ethnography, cooperative prototyping, mock-ups, card sorting, storyboarding, walkthroughs, organizational visits, notes, thematic seminars, and six thinking hats (Ishida, 2012; Kang et al., 2015;

Pedell et al., 2014; Scandurra et al., 2008). Multiple context-appropriate tools and processes that are linked together in a sequence are needed in various phases and for various purposes. Different tools and techniques can allow participants to express the same thing both differently and with different clarity. Tools can serve as activation to potentially provide the basis to contribute to the discussion and to influence how information becomes available in short-term memory (Bonito, 2007). Some tools, such as text, voice, and video can be more appropriate to capture tacit knowledge (a major challenge with Indigenous groups) (Ayub et al., 2018). Some might be more appropriate to support a continuous cycle of learning (McCarthy, 1985), and some such as annotation, orthographic, and perspective illustration and sample images (mood boards) might stimulate information sharing by establishing a sense of ownership (Torrens and Newton, 2013).

Some means of information sharing such as microblogging might require people to get used to new means of communication technology and some participatory design projects need to allow for intergenerational preferences.

## 5.3.2    ENABLERS AND CHALLENGES

A wide spectrum of variables, including external and internal influences, participants' perspectives, and other factors have been reported to either support or hinder participation during participatory design (Chow et al., 1999; Zanotti and Palomino-Schalscha, 2016). This is also noted in Chapter 3. Information sharing is triggered and shaped by the purpose and goals of projects, contexts, and participant composition. Some contexts are more complex than others and in highly complex contexts the information sharing can be more intensive with greater urgency. A few key enablers and challenges are discussed here in more detail.

> **Trust:** Information sharing is influenced by a culture of mutual trust and respect, equality, and freedom of expression and support for a social constructivist learning environment for growth and development (i.e., a Third Space). A conflict and domination-free environment would be ideal (Bergold and Thomas, 2012). Diversity in the composition of participants in participatory design activities who do not know each other and who have often not collaborated before makes it more challenging to develop trust. Even if extra effort is made to enable participants to feel comfortable sharing (Byrne and Sahay, 2007) participants may have concerns about losing control or ownership of their ideas and contributions. Indigenous groups, for example, often struggle with issues of ownership (Zemits et al., 2015).

> **Participant composition:** Findings from team-decision making noted the effects of group composition and people's task-related knowledge and cognitive ability on information sharing, conflict, and group decision effectiveness (Devine, 1999) and how these impact cognitive switching and task self-efficacy (Zha et al., 2019). Adaptive

information sharing is influenced by other people's use, discrepancies, and deliberate initiatives (Zha et al., 2019). Participants are not equally active in sharing information and sometimes motivation mechanisms are needed. In work on team decision-making, it was found that task demonstrability, discussion structures, and cooperation enhance information sharing while distribution, informational interdependence, and member heterogeneity can detract from team information sharing (Mesmer-Magnus and DeChurch, 2009). Cohesion, decision satisfaction, and knowledge integration are also important in team information sharing (Mesmer-Magnus and DeChurch, 2009). Group rewards and group composition can stimulate information sharing directly and can act as a substitute for both epistemic and prosocial motivation (Kang et al., 2015; Super et al., 2016; Zha et al., 2019). Intrinsic motivation is also important (Danielsson and Wiberg, 2006). Cultural intelligence, cultural openness, and self-efficacy significantly influence team member knowledge sharing willingness in cross-national virtual teams (Collins et al., 2017). Awareness and recognition of tensions between actors in specific stakeholder categories during participation due to differences in expectations, strategies, perspectives, experiences, opinions, and domain knowledge are vital. Inter-professional differences in the approach taken to information sharing and the ways professions interrelate might influence information sharing to be "ideal," "over-open," "over-cautious," or "chaotic" (Richardson and Asthana, 2005).

**Personal networks and relationships**: Connections and relationships between people can be enablers or challenges. Widén-Wulff et al. (2008) consider the favorable influence of social environment and social networks on knowledge production. This can be considered with socio-cultural barriers to information seeking noted by Savolainen (2016a), e.g., language problems.

**Roles and tasks:** Research in information behavior has found that roles, tasks, and to some extent responsibilities influence people's information-seeking behavior (Byström and Hansen, 2005; Case and Given, 2016; Vakkari, 1999). Differences have also been noted in roles assigned in collaborative information seeking (Prekop, 2002). We could not find reported evidence of differences in participatory design activities, apart from the fact that participants can be involved in different roles and on different levels, e.g., conceptual level (i.e., idea generation and concept development of, e.g., a system or tool); functional level (i.e., assessment and adaptation of a system or tool according to the project purpose and needs) or operational level (Barcellini et al., 2015). Allin et al. (2018) report participant involvement in a participatory design project as co-designers, codevelopers, and key informants. Some were part of an advisory council. Scariot et al. (2012) note another three levels of user involvement, namely:

informative involvement, consultative involvement, and participatory involvement. Some stakeholder categories might only make an occasional contribution during specific phases in the design process (e.g., funding procurement from sponsors). It can, however, be assumed that roles, tasks, and responsibilities could influence information sharing and other information interaction activities. Zilahi and O'Connors (2019), when studying the information sharing between intensive care unit (ICU) staff and general practitioners, found that the sharing and transfer of information were often brief and incomplete, with role players having too little time, underestimating the value of information, and experiencing difficulty in establishing contact between role players. In addition, strategies for optimal information sharing and recognition of the role of role players may lack, or cause problems. Perceptions of the context and values of a project or case may also impact, e.g., the "whole patient journey" and not just a single point in time such as during treatment.

**Phases:** During meetings, co-designers and informants walk through stages of work that typify participatory design processes such as exploration, discovery, and prototyping. For some participants, the act of meeting regularly with peers and researchers during the exploration phase increased awareness of self-management strategies and techniques and some even modified their own behavior based on information shared during meetings (Allin et al., 2018).

**Culture:** People have different ways of knowing; showing their knowledge and information sharing (Foster, 2007) and sometimes gender and cultural differences need to be noted (Chow et al., 1999). Local ways of knowing (Duckles and Moses, 2018) should be acknowledged especially in cross-cultural work (Foster, 2007; Zanotti and Palomino-Schalscha, 2016). This includes knowledge of cultural customs, e.g., Tikanga Maori (Maori customs) (Liley, 2012) and to establish community entrance (Krauss, 2014). In her work on information sharing across cultural boundaries in developmental contexts, using an information behavior lens, Meyer (2009) found that information behavior seems to evolve as a result of the interplay between elements in cultural contexts. Information behavior of indigenous people proved to be the underlying factor that determines the outcome of information sharing across cultural boundaries between literate and oral cultures. She reported marked differences in information behavior of literate and indigenous people that can influence the extent to which information sharing across cultural boundaries can be successfully accomplished. In some contexts, there might be issues of representation, translation in a broader sense and interpretation (Zanotti and Palomino-Schalscha, 2016). Cultural differences and acculturation may also influence information sharing (Salter and

Schulz, 2005). Cultural values of individualism and collectivism and to a lesser extent power distance can explain national differences in information sharing, and influence behavior in negotiations with incomplete information (Valenzuela et al., 2004). In some cultural groups, there is evidence of multiple consciousnesses and natural connections (Bell et al., 2000) that might contribute to a stronger bond between participants' organizational information cultures. Information practices might also have an impact (Widén and Hansen, 2012). Yeh (2007) argues that we can apply the concepts of information fullness and emptiness to view the relationship between culture and human information behavior. This could also consider habitus, tradition, and prejudice. Challenges might e.g., be experienced in defining content, and processes suiting various parties (Zemits et al., 2015) especially when indigenous identities need to be protected. Zemits et al. (2015) used storytelling to maintain *that Yolŋu identity* in a participatory design project with Australian Aboriginal (*Yolŋu*) communities in northeast Arnhem Land. Dialogue and negotiation and not only information sharing was needed.

**Multiple intelligences:** Gardner's (1983) work and his theory of multiple intelligences alert us to different intelligences that if appropriately acknowledged and understood can enrich the value of input from all stakeholders in the participatory process. He strongly argued for such intelligences, including musical-rhythmic, visual-spatial, verbal-linguistic, logical-mathematical, bodily kinesthetic, interpersonal, intrapersonal, naturalistic, existential, and moral intelligences, not to be compartmentalized. This argument is echoed in more recent work by Martin (2006). Multiple intelligences are also noted in research on participatory design and to a limited extent in research on information sharing or information seeking per se. Recent work on multiple intelligences and participatory design emphasizes design intelligence (D'Souza, 2006), appreciative intelligence (Sandu, 2017), and cultural intelligence (Maggio, 2018). The latter also features in research on information sharing—especially with regard to virtual teamwork and interaction (Collins et al., 2017; Eisenberg and Mattarelli, 2017; Presbitero, 2016).

There are, however, various questions that could not be answered: how does the environment, context, and participatory design participant dynamics influence participants' socio-cognitive experiences, what are the dynamics between the users, designers, and other stakeholders, how does affective experiences impact on information sharing, and how does age gaps in intergenerational projects influence information sharing? Also, what happens with creativity, design proficiency, and participants' ability to cooperate and their artistic abilities? There are many more similar questions to be answered.

### 5.3.3    DYNAMICS OF INFORMATION SHARING IN PARTICIPATORY DESIGN

Participatory design is an endogenous design process introducing external aspects and invisible influencers such as interpersonal dynamics, power relations, cultural capacity, and social positioning that shape negotiation and information sharing during the design process (Bang and Vossoughi, 2016). Participants' involvement and self-expression are very important during participation. They require a sense of: (a) communality; (b) individuality; (c) comfort; (d) health; (e) novelty; and (f) conventionality (Mäkelä and Helfenstein, 2016). Self-affirmation may impact interpersonal discussion, information seeking, and knowledge (Demetriades and Walter, 2016) and so can practical and cultural factors (Zilahi and O'Connor's, 2019). The dynamics in participatory design activities are very complex. Such dynamics influence not only information and knowledge sharing, but also other processes such as sense-making, information synthesis, and information processing. A Third Space may facilitate such dynamics and creative abilities.

## 5.4    FINDINGS ON OTHER INFORMATION ACTIVITIES IN PARTICIPATORY DESIGN AND RELATED CONTEXTS

Although information sharing is the most prominent information activity in participatory design, co-design, and joint decision-making, many other information and especially interaction activities have been noted. Various information activities can be performed to obtain information such as information seeking (Kuhlthau, 1991), information searching (Ellis, 1989), as well as accidentally coming across information (i.e., information encountering) (Erdelez, 1999, 2004; Somerville and Howard, 2010). Somerville and Howard (2010) talk about appreciative inquiry. One part of information sharing can actually be interpreted as information gathering or collection, which is securing information from participants, e.g., on their information needs such as in the project reported by Scandurra et al. (2008) on the use of multidisciplinary thematic seminars in a user needs analysis.

Information encountering is seldom explicitly noted in participatory design literature. Exceptions are the work of information behavior researchers such as Karen Fisher and her co-workers (Fisher et al., 2004, 2013, 2014a, 2014b) and Awan et al. (2019). They report that sharing of encountered information does not always come naturally—it needs to be encouraged. This is interesting since information encountering is strongly associated with serendipity (Conole et al., 2010; Erdelez, 1999) that is prominent in creativity and innovation—two key features of participatory design. Information grounds are perfect places to encounter information.

Staying abreast of new information, e.g., through current awareness services has been noted as necessary in any form of collaborative information seeking (Attfield et al., 2010). They found that the selection, re-aggregation, and forwarding of information by multiple actors give rise to a complex sociotechnical distribution network. Participants may, however, be faced with multiple situational relevance factors in a situation fraught with information overload and restrictive time-pressures.

Communication plays a vital role in participatory information interactions and especially information sharing (Hasell, 1987). This is followed by information processing and cognitive processing (Bonito, 2007; Super et al., 2016; Zha et al., 2019), especially during decision-making (Devine, 1999; Toma and Butera, 2009; Uitdewilligen and Waller, 2018). Distinctive communicative phases have been noted if there are substantial differences between participants, e.g., high- and low-performing teamwork (Schaap et al., 2013). Processes of communication and information processing are also pivotal in information sharing. Since the process of communication influences the quantity and quality of information mentioned during discussions, activation, and choices are important in communication (Bonito, 2007). Activation influences how information becomes available in short-term memory to potentially provide the basis to contribute to the discussion between participants. Choice concerns the conditions under which participants contribute or withhold active information (Bonito, 2007).

Recognition of the purpose and requirements of the design project and negotiation in this regard is essential "to avoid drifting between ad-hoc user wishes and approvals and help users get to the core" of what the purpose, needs, and wants are (Bødker and Iversen, 2002, p. 17). Constant reflection can help to keep focus and to ensure adherence to the purpose of the project, the context, design needs, and participatory design practice and principles (Bødker and Iversen, 2002).

## 5.5    THIRD SPACE: FROM INFORMATION SHARING TO NEW KNOWLEDGE AND CREATIVITY

In participatory design, stakeholders communicate, share information, and address the challenges they experience in a Third Space. They share information to move through this Space where they define and redefine goals, visions, and objectives; reflect on and reconsider their motivations; construct new meanings; bridge gaps in their knowledge and understanding; make sense; redefine their interpretations of the goals of a project; come to new insights and new solutions; adopt new paths of action; and inspire creativity. Here they require congruence between the perceptions of all stakeholders (Könings et al., 2014), and here stakeholders, through information sharing, learn mutually and form new knowledge, ideas, and visions. There is some knowledge of information sharing and other information interaction activities in participatory design activities. This does not extend to the intricacies of how information sharing, and information and cognitive processing are interrelated, or to the equilibrium strategies of participants in different types of interaction and the effect on information sharing, as these manifest in a Third Space. Although research has been done on communication in Third Space (Wagner and Ikas, 2008), this is not explicitly linked to participatory design and information sharing. There might even be the need to explore other information interactions and new types of information objects or artifacts through participatory design highlighting that we may study the process of how information is created and generated and that its conditions are something very novel. It is thus not just about "how information is shared," but also about "how information is created."

## 5.6    SUMMARY

Information sharing in participatory design activities is an essentially continuous, iterative, and cyclic process appearing in design thinking, problem solving, and design creativity. It relies on insider and outsider information and knowledge, influenced by time and timing, movement and pausing, awareness and space, and the ability to create and formulate advances in both design and usage of systems and services from the current ones. Through their creative activities, new knowledge, values, and envisioned practices are unfolded. Information sharing is also essential for mutual learning, development of new knowledge, and reaching mutual understanding (Conole et al., 2010). To deepen understanding of information sharing in a participatory design supported Third Space, appropriate research lenses that can probe information behavior, information practice, collaborative information behavior, and constructivist learning are essential. The same would apply to other information interaction activities and terms often used interchangeably with information sharing such as information exchange, information transfer, information giving, and information distribution. In the next chapter, we focus on the proposed TSIB study framework and the design of new information objects.

# CHAPTER 6

# Third Space as an Intersection Zone for Information Behavior Studies

The value of participatory design has been noted earlier—especially when the creative and constructivist value of Third Space is embraced to allow all participants to have a voice to share knowledge, views and expectations and the right to be listened to when developing new understandings and new information objects and services.

In this chapter, we show how the reviews of the literature in earlier chapters guided our proposal for a framework where Third Space serves as an intersection zone for the development of a *framework to study information behavior in general* and *information sharing* in particular when infused by participatory design as methodology. Many information behavior activities related to the development of shared meaning and new knowledge surrounding the development of information objects and the planning of information behavior research projects can manifest in Third Space. Our understanding of how this happens is still very limited.

Preceding chapters provide ample detail on the clarification of concepts underlying the development of the TSIB study framework we are suggesting (cf., Chapter 2 for clarification of concepts), participatory design (cf., Chapter 3), Third Space (cf., Chapter 4), and information sharing (cf., Chapter 5). Although the framework can be extended to study all information activities falling under information behavior and information practice as umbrella concepts our focus will be on *information sharing as a core activity* (cf., Chapter 5).

The chapter is structured as follows: Section 6.1 deals with a synthesis of previous chapters (Sections 6.1.1–6.1.3). In Section 6.2, we set the scene of the TSIB study framework supported by participatory methodology, methods, processes, and practices (cf., Figure 6.2).

## 6.1 SYNTHESIS—CONTEXTUALIZATION AND COMPLEXITY

Deploying participatory design methodologies can guide the observation of challenges, the development of new information objects to address these, diversity of collaboration, and it can encourage exploration with new information landscapes. It can guide the development of HCIs in a variety of contexts from highly technological to grassroots and community practices. It may enable researchers to move beyond studies that focus only on information searching, seeking, use of information resources, and other information practices and behavior, to include how people jointly make sense, process, transfer, and learn and how they individually as well as socially construct new meaning and understanding. The methodology may also unfold how new information objects can be envisioned and developed.

Generally, in information behavior activities, information sharing is a major component. Information sharing is also one of the necessary features prominently embedded into participatory design methodologies in all phases, stages, steps, and tasks (cf., Chapter 5). We argue that information sharing mostly manifests in a Third Space as an intersectional zone, where a diversity of information activities contributes to end-users' and stakeholders' (i.e., participants') development, and contribution to a democratic and open sharing process to find new solutions. In participatory design, information sharing is a complex activity and means need to be found to deepen understanding of this complexity in a Third Space. A Third Space can also be approached as an intersection (safe) zone to be supported by participatory methods to guide future studies in information behavior and information practice. The latter is the argument that we want to pursue in this chapter.

In Chapters 3, 4, and 5 the complexity of each of participatory design, Third Space, and information sharing in that methodology and that space was revealed. Participatory design practices and findings were noted and the potential to apply participatory design to the complexity of contexts faced by information behavior and information practice research became evident. We noted gaps in our understanding. To move research forward, all end-users and stakeholders need to be engaged in information behavior research to make larger developments possible that can facilitate the formation of new practices and solutions and new information interventions. Many studies are including diverse user groups (Case and Given, 2016), but not a diversity of stakeholders as used in participatory design projects to plan and execute the information behavior study. Neither are the phases, tools, and techniques and values characteristic of participatory design projects applied. Some refer to the values as a design philosophy (Lyng and Pedersen, 2011). To streamline discussion, we do not cite references in this section; we gained ideas from the sources in the list of references, further reading, and exploring additional web resources. The following subsections form the basis for our argument on how Third Space needs to feature in studies of information sharing applying participatory design as methodology. We want to move from knowledge of participatory design, Third Space, and information sharing in general to an argument to use participatory design and its values, methodology, and processes for information behavior studies in any context and covering all information behavior activities (especially information sharing and information interaction) and also information practices. That is depicted in Figures 6.1a and 6.1b at the end of this section. Sections 6.1.1–6.1.3 capture key findings from preceding chapters as context to the proposed TSIB study framework.

## 6.1.1    PARTICIPATORY DESIGN

Utilizing participatory design methods are characterized by open and democratic values, the involvement of a diversity of multiple, evolving stakeholders, and end-users (i.e., participants such as designers, users of systems and others who can contribute) across disciplines and communities in various stages or phases that may be iterative and nonlinear (cf., Chapter 3). It requires, or rather strives to, *congruence* between the perceptions of all participants, understanding of the context, selection of stakeholders and end-users relevant to the challenge and context, demarcation of the boundaries based on the context, selection, and application of methods supporting participation such as Future Workshops, use of appropriate tools, methods and intricacies, boundary objects, nourishment of a Third Space for information sharing, mutual learning and understanding and new knowledge, and the creation of information objects and other (creative) solutions. As shown in Chapter 3, research on participatory design is well established with guidelines on the methodology, process and activity in a diversity of contexts and problems. Creativity is a requirement and innovation may be a goal-oriented outcome, following the identification of the needs and unmet needs of all participants and in particular end-users and applying the principles of inclusive and universal design. Several design or practice phases have been noted in frameworks (some basic and others detailed and complex) involving a multitude of tasks, sometimes referred to as steps or activities. We are incorporating some of these in the TSIB study framework (cf., Figure 6.2). A key feature is the active involvement and engagement of all participants and not just as objects of study, during all facets relevant to the design project and the context. A wide variety of methods, tools and techniques facilitating information sharing and handling, and object development can be employed.

## 6.1.2  THIRD SPACE

Previous chapters (specifically Chapter 4) revealed the potential of Third Space as an essential multilayered and multidimensional interaction and intersection zone. That zone is both a space for unfolding information behavior *activities* such as information sharing and information interaction as well as a space for activating participative *practices*. The unfolding of these activities happens through methods supported by a participatory design approach for both the *methodology* (and collaboration) and also *activities* such as information sharing and creative activities. The value of the zone or space lies in support for the mutual formation of needs and requirements of end-users/stakeholders, new knowledge, and physical/virtual design practices in order to envision future design, usage, outcomes, and solutions such as information objects. The physical manifestation of the latter is evident in new objects such as information objects. Boundary objects are used to trigger activities such as information sharing. Both a First Space of individual prior knowledge and experience and a Second Space (influenced by society and both individual and group gained knowledge and new learning) forms part of a Third Space interaction space or zone (cf., Figure 6.3). These spaces might take many forms ranging from physical to virtual and cognitive. Third Space forms the boundary region and is marked by borderlines and boundary crossing to navigate differences in the disciplines, cultures, knowledge domains and discourse communities of participants. In Figures 6.1a and 6.1b, Third Space is presented with a dotted line to indicate flexibility and boundary crossing. The product resolution created through participatory design uses one or more *boundary objects* to trigger activities that can result in the creation of an *information object* or other outcome such as another type of object or event. These are also indicated in Figures 6.1a and 6.1b. Participants must experience Third Space as a safe space where they can contribute and where new meaning, sense-making, and knowledge evolve and where they can collaborate in a constructive and constructivist, collaborative manner especially with regard to higher order cognitive functions. A variety of information behavior and especially information sharing activities and practices are at stake and information and access to information sources are key requirements.

### 6.1.3    INFORMATION SHARING

Previous chapters (specifically Chapter 5) revealed that information sharing in projects is complex, multifaceted, and multilayered. It is a core activity that manifests in tandem and symbiotically with individual and collaborative constructivist learning, knowledge forming, and creative activities. (Some of these are depicted in Figure 5.1.) Research of information sharing per se, information sharing as part of collaborative information behavior, and information sharing supported by participative methods, is still inadequate to understand the full complexity of information sharing and the simultaneous and symbiotic or in-tandem relationship between information sharing and other activities. Other fields of study might shed light on such relationships and the activities taking place e.g., Communication, Linguistics, and also research on learning and creativity. Information objects and other material expressions are also shared in Third Space and can range from facts, opinions, ideas, places, feelings, thoughts, and reflections to awareness. Strategic, paradigmatic, directive, and social information can be shared through print, verbal communication, sophisticated technology, artifacts, art, and many other formats. Information sharing happens at different levels: individual, task-related, and discipline (domain) related levels. The function of information sharing must be extended to establish mutual awareness between the person giving information and the person receiving information. Information is shared for different purposes that includes raising consciousness or awareness, building relationships between participants and sharing ideas, thoughts, and emotions, and a variety of tools can be used. There are many challenges in participatory design and many factors can motivate information sharing. In participatory design methodology, boundary objects are used to trigger information sharing in Third Space. This is shown in various figures in this chapter; also, in Figures 6.1a and 6.1b.

Figure 6.1a offers a summary view of participatory design methodology in general and a Third Space intersection where many activities and specifically information sharing, take place. Participatory design as methodology for a project with the purpose to design a new information or other object (cf., Chapter 3) drives the process where a Third Space (cf., Chapter 4) evolves where boundary objects are used and a new object (e.g., an information object) or event is created. The outcome should be at least guidelines for the development of such an object or social event. There are many information behavior activities and especially information sharing activities and information practices as well as other activities such as sense-making and learning (cf., Chapter 5). The scribbling spirals represents ongoing—back and forth—information sharing and other information behavior activities and practices. This emulates the spiral presentation of participatory design in Figure 3.1. Participatory design participants in general include designers, researchers, users, experts from various fields, etc. Figure 6.1.b portrays a very similar situation when participatory design methodology and a Third Space interaction section are applied **when doing information behavior studies**. The planning and execution of the information behavior study is infused by participatory design as methodology to include the values, phases, techniques, and tools of participatory design and especially choices in participants. The planning and execution of the information behavior study happens in the Third Space. This includes negotiating the purpose and goals of the research study, interpreting the literature and findings, and an end product that can take many different forms such as a new theory or model or ideas for further research or recommendations for the design of a new information object. It also involves envisioning future behavior and challenges. In information behavior studies participant selection is in particular important. For an information behavior study, participants' *group composition* considers roles relevant to the *purpose* of the study as well as the *context* of the study, e.g., information behavior researcher(s), designers, all user groups (e.g., students, lecturers, managers), experts in moderating design participation, the Learning Sciences, Linguistics, Communication, etc. In addition, participant group composition should consider the *role* in the context of the information behavior study, e.g., patient, caregiver, or health professional. The *individual participant profiles* need to allow for a diversity of *characteristics* such as educational background, language, culture, age, gender, expertise, skills, and needs. In both figures, boundary objects are shown as *triggers of information sharing* and other activities.

The main difference between Figures 6.1a and 6.1b would be the intended outcome (linked to the purpose and goal), the choice of participants and presumably the nature of information sharing activities that is something to be studied in future. In Figure 6.1b, the outcome is focused on doing research that can lead to a new theory or model or findings that might lead to recommendations for the design of an information object, information service, an information intervention, or even further research.

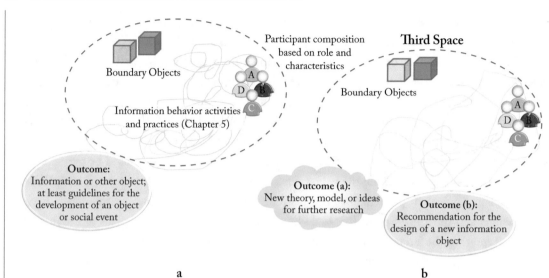

Figure 6.1: (a, b) Applying a participatory design approach to information behavior studies.

Apart from the obvious need to study information behavior and information practices taking place during participatory design projects, we want to propose a TSIB study framework on how participatory design can be used as the *methodology* and the *process* to conduct information behavior research. This would add a value set of openness and collaborative input and a richness of processes and tools that overlaps with what is currently being used in information behavior research, but also new ones not normally employed such as participatory design workshops (cf., Appendix A), and a much richer variety of stakeholders who can participate in planning an information behavior research study.

## 6.2    A TSIB STUDY FRAMEWORK: SETTING THE SCENE

In this section, we argue for a framework to guide information behavior studies and that can deepen insight of information sharing as a core information behavior activity as well as the Third Space of interaction. We first present the framework (cf., Figure 6.2) before discussing two key constructs in more detail: (a) Third Space as an interaction/intersection zone; and (b) information sharing and other information activities.

Many information behavior models can guide studies (Savolainen, 2016b). Some are theoretical and others are derived from empirical studies. Shenton and Hay-Gibson (2012) describe a meta-model as a model that has been derived from one or more existing models. They argue that an information behavior meta-model falls into three categories: (a) those that unify, within one framework, disparate models/theories from a number of areas; (b) those that integrate the fundamentals of several models which share common strands; and (c) those that recast an established model for a particular purpose. If a participatory design methodology approach is applied to information behavior studies it should be able to study an information behavior activity (printed as scribbles in Figures 6.1a and 6.1b and spirals with scribbles) presenting the cyclic nature of information sharing and other activities through all phases and applied to all components in Figure 6.2). In addition, the study would be driven by the values of participatory design to focus on the dynamics of information sharing and information interaction activities in Third Space (including the space of individual prior knowledge and experience) and the space of individual and grouped gained knowledge and new learning.

The proposed TSIB study framework builds on insights gained from the preceding chapters, Figures 6.1a and 6.1b and previous work reported by Meyer et al. (2018, 2020). In Meyer et al. (2020), a nascent framework was presented to guide information behavior studies of participatory design—that is, research on the information activities taking place during a participatory design project. That framework included 12 constructs deducted from a scoping review of participatory design research in educational contexts and information behavior models and frameworks. It allows for the context that can be extended to the environment and for participants (they refer to stake-holder categories and actors—typical terminology in information behavior research). The framework also allows for roles, tasks, levels of participant involvement, and information needs (triggered by the envisaged purpose and outcomes which are refined by participants during the course of the project based on mutual learning and idea generation). In addition, the framework includes iterative processes and phases, stages, and steps and intervening variables (although there are many such variables, domain knowledge, expertise and prior knowledge stand out). Lastly, the nascent framework by Meyer et al. (2020) allowed for information sources and access to information; information activities, especially sharing, seeking, organization, encountering and communication, and techniques and tools.

The TSIB study framework (Figure 6.2) builds on the previous framework, but now moves towards applying participatory design as methodology to conduct an information behavior study in any context. Although many of the same issues apply, the focus is different. For purposes of the TSIB study framework, *Third Space* represents the intersection zone where constructivist activities and strategies, sense-making, learning, and mutual learning occur (cf., Figure 5.1). *Third Space* becomes the center (Figure 6.3). Here the information behavior study is planned and executed applying participatory design as methodology and here the information behavior activities that must be studied manifest in addition to the information behavior of the end-user group being researched. The framework in Figure 6.2 should guide information behavior studies infused by participatory design methodology.

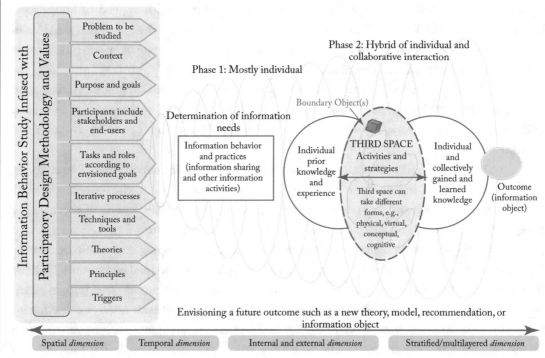

Figure 6.2: Information behavior studies enriched with participatory design methodology.

From the processes or tasks typical to applying participatory design methodology (cf., Chapter 3), the following seems appropriate to information behavior studies; these are not applied in a linear fashion and are often iterative and cyclic and are marked by cyclic manifestations of information behavior and information practices (more detail in Section 6.2.2) and especially the activities and interactions in Third Space—the interactive zone (more detail in Section 6.2.1).

- Demarcation of the information behavior problem to investigate.

- Demarcation and consideration of the context of the study; that will include the environment in which the information behavior problem will be studied such as geographic region. This is not shown in Figure 6.2. A study may be contextualized depending on for example, domain, user population and geographical limitations and can also be described as the zone of focus. A study needs to include contextual inquiries.

- Determination of the purpose and goals of the information behavior study.

- Determination, selection, and involvement of participants that will include stakeholders and end-users and for information behavior research specifically those who can add no insights to the planning of the study such as experts in participatory design, communication, the learning sciences, and the context per se.

- Determination and definition of participant needs, requirements, and information needs—in particular the needs of end-users.

- Determination of tasks and roles according to the envisioned purpose and goals.

- Execution of iterative processes such as brainstorming, information searching, and information-sharing processes in which information may be used to create information objects.

- Application of participatory design techniques and tools to elicit input and information sharing from all participants.

- Consideration of appropriate information behavior theories (Fisher, Erdelez, and McKenzie, 2006) as well as theories from other disciplines such as the learning and communication sciences.

- Consideration and possible application of principles for participation and co-creation such as inclusion, empathy, and learning from each other.

- Use of a variety of triggers such as boundary objects to stimulate information sharing and creative thinking and activities.

- Envisioning a future outcome such as a new theory, model, recommendation, or information object. The use study (cf., Section 6.3) gives an example.

In the TSIB study framework (cf., Figure 6.2) we foresee the activities as cyclic, cylindrical circles that are filled with scribbles. The information behavior activities already start during the information behavior researcher's conceptualization of the problem and the planning stages such as observing the problem or doing a literature survey. This is indicated as Phase 1 in Figure 6.2 and entails mostly individual activities. Information sharing in "prior" steps can include selecting the research problem, determining context, and selecting participants, as shown in Figure 6.2. Once this is done, the collaboration and Third Space interaction can start. Interaction with colleagues and team members are not excluded. Phase 2 concerns a hybrid of *individual prior knowledge and information* and *individual and collaborative interaction*. Information sharing happens through all the phases and applies to all components. When applying a participatory design methodology an essential difference with how information behavior studies is normally conducted, is how the values of participatory design can ensure the freedom, safe space, and encouragement for all participants to have a voice throughout all the steps of an information behavior research project.

Two constructs are of particular importance for the application of the framework: (a) Third Space's potential interaction and the role of participants; and (b) information sharing and other information activities.

### 6.2.1    THIRD SPACE, POTENTIAL INTERACTION, AND THE ROLE OF PARTICIPANTS

Third Space as an interaction zone is marked by several characteristics, one being the role taken on by participants and how they interact. Figure 6.3 represents Third Space and its elements as a potential zone of interaction, and Figure 6.4 represents the interaction between participants. This zone is situated in a context and environment that are not reflected in the sketch.

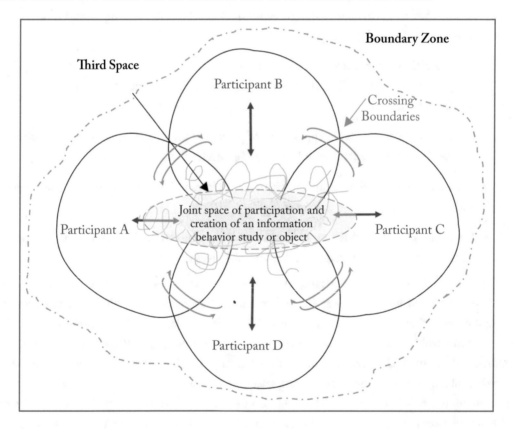

Figure 6.3: Third Space potential interaction between participants.

Several elements in Figure 6.3 require further explanation: context; contextual spaces; participants (including composition, interaction, and determination of needs); information activities; boundary zones, and boundary crossing; intersectional zone; and outcomes.

- **Environment:** Environment can refer to a geographical region, institution, or even virtual environment where the information behavior study will be conducted. The environment is depicted as the solid blue line in Figure 6.3.

- **Context and contextual spaces:** All information behavior studies and all participatory design projects relate to a specific context such as an educational or health setting, problem domain, or a bigger environment such as a rural area or specific country; this is the contextual space of the study. The Third Space manifests in this contextual space. There is an *external space* that represents the larger and general problem domain and setting; this is represented by the dotted circle in Figure 6.3 and the *internal space* (full circle) that represents the more *concrete* and *targeted* space or zone that becomes the *intersection zone* of the problem, e.g., planning and conducting an information behavior study. The internal space operates with both concrete and abstract spaces. That can be physical, virtual, or hybrid spaces (or combinations of these) of interaction and cognitive; conceptual and other abstract spaces might develop. We did not attempt to draw these details into Figure 6.3. A variety of participants take part; in general, this will include the information behavior researcher(s), experts in participatory design or other design experts depending on the nature of the information behavior project, and also the people whose information behavior is studied such as the users of an information system, students, or patients. Third Space is the joint space of interaction and creation. This can be the planning and execution of an information behavior study and in some situations such a study might lead to the need to follow participatory design methodology to design a new information object (cf., Figure 6.1b). In Third Space there is extensive interaction between participants. That is indicated by the scribbles and the arrows showing interactions between participants which can be individuals or end-users or stakeholder groups. In Figure 6.3, the use of boundary objects is not portrayed. The crossing of boundaries is shown as a very important and distinguishing characteristic of Third Space. This means referral to the fact that participants in an information behavior research project (i.e., those who lead the study and those who will interpret the results and those who are the stakeholders or end-users being studied) need to interact with people from other disciplines and professional backgrounds. They have to learn new terminology, different ways of thinking about a problem. They will move between different disciplinary perspectives, e.g., if information scientists and librarians are working with doctors and nurses and social workers on an information portal for patients, there will be *at least five* disciplinary perspectives. To this can be added the voices and perspectives of experts in HCI and even instructional designers as experts in teaching and learning. Much more detail would be at stake in a typical information behavior study. The composition of the participants and specifically the stakeholders as stated before, will depend on the contexts. There might also be different cultural identities, languages, and generational differences when older as well as younger participants are involved. The nature of the boundaries crossed will depend on the participant composition.

- **Participants including composition, interaction, determination of needs, and roles:** When an information behavior study applies participatory design as methodology it is important to involve all user groups for the context and purpose of the study. If the purpose is to provide information services to cancer patients the patients and caregivers, family members, doctors, nurses, social workers, dieticians, clergy, etc., should be involved in the planning as appropriate to the specific problem being studied. Information behavior research has pointed towards many differences between these groups (Case and Given, 2016; Fourie, 2008). In addition to ensuring that sharing of information meets with the values of participatory design, expertise in the facilitation of the planning of the study and actually doing the study is required. To understand deeper meanings of words, gestures, and to prompt sharing of information expertise in questioning, negotiation, and team decision-making as well as reflection, creativity, and learning is required. These are especially important if the purpose is to deepen theoretical insight and not just the development of an information object. The composition of stakeholders and the participant profiles (cf., Chapter 5 for influencing characteristics) is very important. They need to bring different expertise to the study and will include end-users of the outcome or people affected by the information behavior study, e.g., refugees, patients, or students (i.e., the people whose information behavior needs to be studied). In information behavior contexts participants are sometimes also referred to as actors (Meyer et al., 2020). Each of the participants have different *roles* during the study, requiring different information activities. These roles also include the role of moderator, researcher, and designer. All participants involved are assumed to contribute with their knowledge, experience, and envisioning. Figure, 6.1a, and 6.1b present the position of participants in a participatory design project and Figure 6.3 shows participant positions in the contextual, Third Space. Although the figure portrays only four participants, any number of people can be involved. Participant composition may also change during a project and one project might result into the next, as shown in Figure 6.6. Various interactions or dynamics may occur as depicted in the scenarios in Figure 6.4.

- **Participant interaction and acknowledging participant needs, requirements, and information needs:** In sharing knowledge from different domains, bringing cultural identity and complexity to the Third Space interaction zone, and adding different discipline perspectives that contribute to blending discourses, interaction can take different forms. The immense complexity of such interaction leaves much scope for further research. Each of the participating people with their roles also represent implicit and explicit user needs and user requirements—that is, needs that must be fulfilled through (a) the outcome of the information behavior study guided by participatory design methodology, and (b) needs that must be fulfilled in conducting the information behavior study. The needs are triggered by the envisaged purpose and outcomes of the research project which are refined by participants during the course of the project based on mutual learning and idea generation (manifesting in Third Space and involving both individual prior knowledge and the new individual and group learning). Furthermore, the needs and requirements may be operationalized through defining and constructing different types of tasks, work tasks, and leisure tasks. These tasks are being defined, activated, and performed in order to reveal the necessary problems, short-comings, proposals for ideas, and solutions (cf., Chapter 3 for more detail on the methodology and processes of participatory design). Although roles and tasks are often considered as intervening variables in information behavior research, Meyer et al. (2020) decided to present these as separate constructs with levels of participant involvement due to their prominence in participatory design projects. Boundary objects, participatory design tools, and methods are used to help to determine user needs and requirements. As noted in Chapter 5, this is not an easy process and researchers need to draw on the wealth of information behavior literature in this regard for further reading (e.g., Case and Given, 2016). From information behavior research, it is clear that there are still many problems in identifying dormant information needs and to work through the different levels on which information needs are often recognized and expressed (Shenton, 2007; Taylor, 1968). Without going into further details, it is clear that the interaction between participants in Third Space and in particular the determination of needs and information needs are core issues requiring further research. Figure 6.4 portrays (a) different scenarios of the boundary object in relation to the individual spaces of the participants, and (b) the different overlaps of individual spaces that may occur when gathering different people together. The figure shows the different levels of complexity when it comes to the different combinations of the Third Space settings.

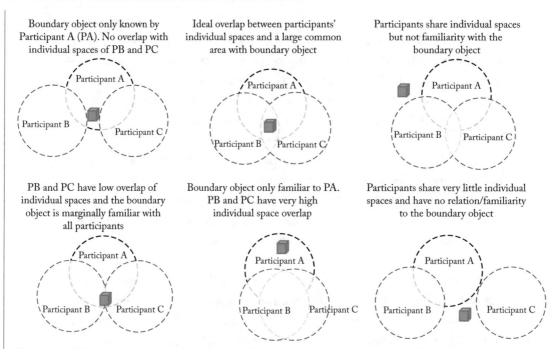

Figure 6.4: Envisaged scenarios for what can happen between participants in Third Space.

- **Information activities:** In connection with the needs and requirements, the participants will establish a set of goals and future applications of the creative and information activities. A wide spectrum of information activities as well as other activities such as sense-making, learning, and creating happens in Third Space. These are presented as scribbles in Figures 6.2 and 6.3. These activities are discussed in the next section and portrayed in more detail in Figure 6.5.

- **Boundary zones and boundary crossing:** As explained in Chapter 4, boundary zones and boundary crossing are at the core of Third Space and essential. The crossing of boundaries can be on an intellectual, cultural, social, political, or other level and can be figuratively or abstract. The Third Space intersection zone should support and encourage such crossing. It is essential for creative endeavors.

- **Intersectional zone:** In Chapter 4, Third Space is noted as an in-between space that is created at intersections. Thus, forming an intersection zone for interaction. These intersections can be material, discursive, or metaphoric between an individual's prior knowledge and gained knowledge from participatory activities.

## 6.2.2   INFORMATION SHARING AND OTHER INFORMATION BEHAVIOR ACTIVITIES IN THIRD SPACE

As explained in Chapter 5 and shown in Figure 6.5, information activities happen in tandem and in a symbiotic relationship to many other activities such as positioning activities, learning activities, cognition activities, reflective activities and participative activities. There are certainly many more. These activities, the relationship with information activities and information behavior and information practices offer fertile ground for further research. In Figure 6.5, we portray some of the activities and we focus on the different dimensions of information sharing. All of these would apply to the different phases where information activities manifest (cf., Figure 6.2), e.g., the prior, First Phase (selecting the research problem, determining context, and selecting participants) and the Second Phase with both individual activities and collaboration in Third Space.

In a Third Space, activities range from information activities to learning, creative, and emotional activities. On a more specific level, that can include information seeking, searching, retrieval, sharing, interaction, organization, management, avoidance and encountering, and communication, as well as selecting information sources and using information handling tools such as search engines, as well as other actions such as talking, writing, sketching, taking pictures, and also arguing, negotiating, and stressing, getting angry, and experiencing a sense of achievement. There are many more that need to be investigated with reference to the dynamics and movement through the Third Space and the goals that are envisioned based on current information activities and in response toward future and envisioned solutions. Some of the activities are noted in Figures 5.1 and 6.5. Information can be information as thing (data or an object or source), information as knowledge or information as process (Buckland, 1991). Apart from information sharing and other information behavior activities and practices, there are many other activities at stake in Third Space as a constructivist and creative space (cf., Chapter 5, Figure 5.1, and Figure 6.5). We will not elaborate on these. We specifically note the following dimensions in Figure 6.5 that need attention in an information behavior study: spatial dimension, temporal dimension, internal and external dimension and stratified or multilayered dimension (cf., Figure 6.5). There may be more.

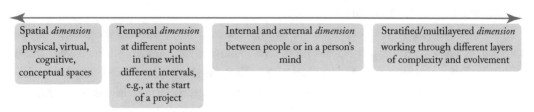

Figure 6.5: Typical participant activities taking place in Third Space.

- **Spatial dimension:** this is the dimension where participants work in and experience different spaces such as working in a physical environment such as an office or laboratory or on a virtual platform. Participants also work in different cognitive and conceptual spaces where their understanding of the problem that is investigated in the information behavior study changes and where they redefine their interpretations of terminology, the literature they are using and possibly even research methods.

- **Temporal dimension**: all participatory activities where participants fulfill their roles and take different actions, and where they are involved in different tasks at different stages of the information behavior research study manifests at different intervals of the project (i.e., the information behavior study) and for different durations. Participants will have different experiences and possibly different intensities of these as a participatory design methodology is applied to conduct the study, e.g., differences at the start of the project and definition of the problem and then later at the stages of actually doing the research, collecting data, and analyzing and interpreting the data.

- **Internal and external dimension:** different activities can manifest between participants or only in an individual person's mind. The latter applies to each participant and can also have temporal dimensions.

- **Stratified/multilayered dimension**: in an information behavior study, participants need to work through various levels of complexity. The exact nature of this dimension needs to be determined by further research when applying the TSIB study framework that we are proposing in Figure 6.2.

In the TSIB study framework, we allow for different tools, techniques, and materials—boundary objects—to be used to activate and in some cases trigger communication, interaction, information sharing, understanding and exchanging of experiences among all participants. Such triggers or boundary objects cannot only initiate interactivities, but can also shape interactivities. This is another fertile field for further research.

As a result of an information behavior study, there might be different outcomes as suggested in Figure 6.1b namely recommendations for further research, a new mode, and framework and theory. In Figure 6.6 this is represented by Outcome 1. There might also be a recommendation for the design of a new object such as Outcome 1.1. In order to design the latter, the creative participative process will continue in an iterative way applying relevant information methods.

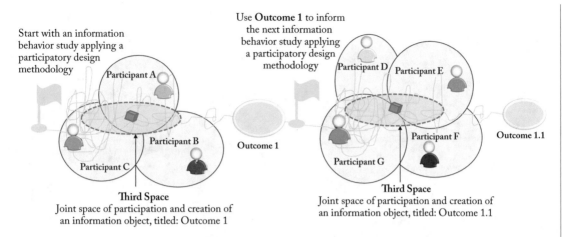

Figure 6.6: Outcomes of an information behavior study applying a participatory design methodology might lead to additional information objects (outcomes).

## 6.3   SUMMARY

In this chapter, we presented a new and innovative framework to guide information behavior studies that can address the deep challenges faced by contemporary society as sketched in the Preface and Chapter 1. We reiterated the value of Chapters 2, 3, 4, and 5 in shaping our insight and the framework we propose. The TSIB study framework intends to infuse information behavior research with tools and perspectives from participatory design as methodology and process. Most importantly, the rich composition of a diversity of participants contributing to the planning, development and execution of an information behavior study, a Third Space where interaction and stimulation with boundary objects, and a variety of tools and techniques is nurtured. And further, more awareness to study information sharing and other activities and to address the challenges faced by society and the needs of all groups. In the next chapter, we offer some use-case studies that can inspire the application of the model and further work in information behavior research leading to innovative and creative design of information objects.

CHAPTER   7

# Conclusion and the Way Forward

In this book, we started by considering the research and findings on the following: (a) participatory design as methodological approach and process; (b) Third Space as an essential zone of observing information interaction and intersection in participatory projects, as well as other fields such as education and information literacy training; and (c) findings of information sharing as a core information behavior activity that manifest with many other activities. There are many opportunities for further research and especially for studies on the nature and scope of information behavior during participatory projects as we also observed in earlier work (Meyer et al., 2020).

From the outset, we expressed concern for the numerous challenges in contemporary society that can benefit from applying participatory design especially because of its value set and range of tools and techniques that can be used and also the processes exploring a Third Space for information sharing and other information activities. We also noted the challenges contemporary society faces that require information behavior research on a more intensive scale, searching for deeper understanding and insight that can lead to information related solutions that can address more varied information needs and preferences and that can lead to more creative and appropriate information objects and opportunities that can meet such needs. Third Space is especially conducive to the creativity that is required for such work.

In the TSIB study framework (cf., Figure 6.2), we explained how the choice of participants in the planning and conduction of information behavior research will be impacted and how Third Space, the use of boundary objects, consideration of context and situated awareness, boundary crossing and the dynamics between information sharing and other information behavior and activities such as learning will be impacted.

This book is intended to bring together students and scholars from areas such as information behavior and information seeking, as well as from information science and HCI, and other related disciplines such as informatics and education to further explore the Third Space in different contexts, domains and application areas. Our focus is on understanding information sharing in such initiatives and to show how information behavior studies can be enhanced by a participatory design approach, and also, how any other participatory design studies can get a deeper awareness and understanding of information behavior and information practices that manifest during such design work.

The interaction and dynamics between information sharing and other activities is important. For each of these, there is considerable detail to flesh out and also scope for further research—that is not the purpose of this book. Although participatory design can serve as the practical and facilitative support to study information behavior it must be supported by theories and frameworks from information behavior, information practice, and the learning sciences (cf., Chapter 5). In addition, theoretical insight is especially needed to explore the different spaces in Third Space (i.e., the spatial dimension), time and timing (i.e., temporal dimension and temporality), movement and progress between layers of complexity (i.e., the stratified dimension), internal and external dimension, fluency and fluidity, different types of awareness such as spatial awareness, cognitive spatial awareness and emotional spatial awareness, action and dormancy in information sharing and latent creativity in Third Space. Theories related to constructivist learning and sense-making also need to be identified and explored.

Systematic reviews and critical interpretive synthesis of theoretical lenses in relation to information behavior studies and participatory design might be other good points of departure. Apart from theories noted in Chapter 5, we will not try to identify other theoretical lenses.

For the future, both practical applications of the TSIB study framework—exploration of theoretical grounds and research gaps—need to be addressed. We are offering a few suggestions and two use cases to demonstrate how the TSIB study framework can be applied and how interdisciplinary and transdisciplinary collaboration is supported. The use cases illustrated that there is ample scope for further research.

## 7.1    SUGGESTIONS FOR PRACTICAL APPLICATIONS OF THE TSIB STUDY FRAMEWORK

Basically, the application of the TSIB study framework is about framing specific research settings. Although it does not prescribe specific methods of data collection and data analysis involved, it does suggest activities supported by the participatory design approach and the role of the stakeholders—the participants—in making such activities. Throughout the book we clearly suggest a human-centered approach to information behavior and information seeking activities, with a focus on information behavior as creative and on learning processes involving participation and engagement as key activities. Our intention is, however, not to suggest any specific measures that need to be performed.

Although there may be many opportunities for practical applications of the TSIB study framework, we highlight only a few: applying the framework in complex contexts facing deep challenges such as in healthcare, grief, and bereavement, any context related to the information challenges faced by marginalized groups, as well as sophisticated technological contexts. Such challenges are sketched in more detail in Chapter 1. Applying the TSIB framework in new spaces such as the spaces created over the Internet, web camera telecasts, video conferencing services, chat rooms with video audio chatting, blogging, and, most recently, online social networking offers many opportunities. Thus, applying the TSIB study framework in spaces advancing beyond the inadequacy of dualism, as in physical and mental spaces. The framework can also be used to study various activities (such as learning activities, cognition activities, reflective activities, participative activities, positioning activities, creative activities, and emotional activities) taking place in the creation of different information objects.

Looking ahead, the development of new social environments such as artificial intelligence, immersive technologies such as augmented reality (Xiao et al., 2020), virtual reality (Li et al., 2019; Lou et al., 2020a, 2020b), and big data will result in the need for new knowledge to be constructed and combined with existing knowledge, thus also transforming how we view, create, apply, and collaborate in Third Spaces, and may imply the rise of new spaces (e.g., Morisson, 2018).

Further investigation is needed into the specific conditions required for the formation of a Third Space as an intersection zone, as well as how these specific conditions impact different information activities. Further research is also required on the balance in the dynamics between sharing, learning, creativity and designing of information services, tools and objects, the influence of movement or progress, and the impact of multiple intelligences among stakeholders (cf., Chapter 5).

Against this background of opportunities, we present two practical examples—use cases—of how the TSIB study framework can be applied in information behavior studies: (a) a health information behavior study of cancer prevention in deep rural South Africa; and (b) the digital diary memory table—a public information device in a blended space. Although the examples refer to the literature to acknowledge ideas collected from reported studies, they do not present studies that have actually been executed, but suggest scenarios utilizing our TSIB framework and its elements. The context and purpose of an information behavior study will influence how the framework is applied. The use cases will illustrate the application of participatory elements and processes supporting information behavior studies using the TSIB study framework suggested in Figures 6.2 and 6.3. Use case 1 will focus strongly on the diversity of participants to include when doing cross-cultural research with marginalized communities. Use case 2 will elaborate more closely on the parts that deal with participants and their needs and their relationship with the boundary zones and objects and interactional zones. The goal with these examples is to highlight part of the information behavior process that especially involve participatory aspects to be considered.

## 7.1.1    USE CASE 1: CANCER PREVENTION IN DEEP RURAL SOUTH AFRICA

This use case focuses on marginalized contexts, namely an information behavior study to determine how the need for cervical cancer screening can be best communicated to women in deep rural areas in South Africa (a developing country with both poor and affluent communities; deep rural areas and world class cities). Deep rural refers to areas who may not have electricity or Internet connectivity except through mobile technology. Cervical cancer is a female cancer falling under gynecological cancers (Westbrook and Fourie, 2015). According to Figure 6.2, the following must be considered.

**Demarcation of the information behavior problem to investigate:** The information behavior researcher or a group of research collaborators will determine and demarcate the problem to be solved as the point of departure, e.g., How can the need for cervical cancer screening be best communicated to women in deep rural areas in South Africa?

**Demarcation and consideration of the context of the study:** A study may be contextualized depending on, e.g., the domain, user population and environment such as geographical location. In this case the domain will be cervical cancer; that is a female cancer falling under gynecological cancers (Westbrook and Fourie, 2015). The user population will be women. (Some cancers typically associated with women such as breast cancer, may also affect men. The population composition should thus not be taken for granted.) The population might further be demarcated in terms of age and ethnic groups. The geographic region is South Africa—a developing country with a diversity of Indigenous ethnic groups and 11 official languages. Research has reported that some Indigenous languages such as isiXhosa, do not even have appropriate terminology for cancer treatment such as radiation. "A strong emotional connotation is carried by the word used in isiXhosa for radiation, that is, *ukutshisa/thisa*, which literally means to burn, to set on fire, fuse, scorch" (Lourens, 2013, p. 110). isiXhosa is the prominent language in the Eastern Cape province of South Africa. In KwaZulu-Natal, another province, isiZulu and the Zulu culture and traditions are most prominent. If the context of the study is an oncology treatment center in the affluent suburbs of Johannesburg, the context and participants will be very different.

**Determination of the purpose and goals of the information behavior study:** The researcher(s) will decide on a purpose and goal such as developing information objects in an Indigenous language that can improve cancer prevention. Once participants join the project, the purpose and goals can be refined to include objectives representing views from the participants. Apart from a very practical goal such as the design of booklets or pamphlets, lyrics for rap (music), or a play, academic research studies would also envisage the development of new theories and frameworks and recommendations for further research (Sameshima et al., 2017; Zehbe et al., 2016). These studies provide an interesting perspective from Alaskan experiences with First Nation women.

**Determination, selection, and involvement of participants:** That will include stakeholders and end-users and for information behavior research specifically those who can add new insights to the planning of a research study such as experts in participatory design, communication, the learning sciences and input relevant to the context per se, e.g., oncology nurses or social workers. The researcher(s) will identify stakeholders from an information behavior perspective as well as from the perspective of the context. Apart from information behavior researchers familiar with the South African context, health information seeking, and information transfer in communities with an oral tradition would be useful. End-users can include cancer patients, cancer survivors (i.e., people in cancer remission), and their families. In addition, people from the community who are trusted by end-users and with whom they feel comfortable to engage may be included such as religious and spiritual leaders and traditional healers.

**Determination of tasks and roles according to the envisioned purpose and goals:** Each of the participants have different roles during the study, requiring different information activities. These roles also include the roles of moderator, researcher, and designer, while tasks may include interpretation from the language spoken by end-users and making initial contact with the group (Krauss, 2014) and gaining trust or conducting interviews with patients. Fourie (2008) worked with a social oncology worker to conduct interviews with terminally ill patients and their families.

**Execution of iterative processes such as brainstorming, information searching, and information sharing processes from which information may be used to create information objects:** A number of processes may then follow that can align with the choice of a particular participatory design framework as sketched in Chapter 3. Such processes must meet with the preferences of participants and especially end-users and with respect for cultural differences.

**Application of participatory design techniques and tools to elicit input and in-formation sharing from all participants:** This can include a variety of information activities such as searching databases for relevant literature, a scoping literature review of existing information, consulting with an expert in the language of the end-users, isiXhosa, and using techniques and tools appropriate to the cultural norms and tradi-tions of the participants—particularly the end-users.

**Consideration of appropriate information behavior and other theories:** For this use case, theories on health communication in particular would be useful or empow-ering theory (Hussain et al. 2012).

**Consideration and possible application of principles for participation and co-cre-ation such as inclusion, empathy, and learning from each other:** Researchers need to draw on expertise from participatory design and literature reviews for more ideas e.g., as sketched by Hussain et al. (2012).

**Use of a variety of triggers such as boundary objects to stimulate information sharing and creative thinking and activities:** A boundary object may be familiar to some participants and less so to others, as shown in Figure 6.4. In working with Indigenous communities, culturally appropriate boundary objects need to be identified and used; this would require research into the needs of especially end-users and their cultural background. More conventional boundary objects might be more appropriate for some participants, e.g., doctors, oncology nurses and social workers. The intention with the boundary objects is to stimulate interaction between participants and in particular information sharing. Islind et al. (2019) provide a detailed discussion on boundary objects for heterogeneous studies.

**Awareness and consideration of applicable dimensions such as a spatial dimension, temporal dimension, internal and external dimension, and stratified/multi-layered dimensions:** For this use case, the spatial dimension might include visits to the deep rural areas and tribal villages and dwellings to collect information to present at virtual meetings between other participants who may find themselves in different parts of the world. The temporal dimension might include the time that is required to get entrance into the end-user community and to gain trust with the leaders as well as different times in the progress of the research project. Krauss (2014) provides an excellent discussion on gaining community entrance. It will also include the different phases from the start of the research study and the expectations that dynamics between participants will be very different by the end of the study. Information will be collected within the group of participants or from individual participants' thinking and internalization (i.e., internally) as well as from external sources such as researchers who have worked elsewhere with Indigenous communities (i.e., external dimension). Through the application of the TSIB study framework researchers must realize that different dimensions will have an impact as the project progresses.

**Determination and definition of participant needs, requirements, and information needs—in particular the needs of end-users:** Since studies in health information behavior have found that emotional, care, and supportive needs feature very strongly in the healthcare context, the study might include more than just information needs, e.g., drawing on expertise on affect and emotion (Fourie and Julien, 2014).

**Participant interaction and acknowledging participant needs, requirements, and information needs:** In sharing knowledge from different domains, bringing cultural identity and complexity to the Third Space interaction zone, and adding different disciplinary perspectives that contribute to blending discourses, interaction can take different forms. The immense complexity of such interaction leaves much scope for further research. Each of the participating persons with their roles also represent implicit and explicit user needs and user requirements—that is, needs that must be fulfilled through: (a) the outcome of the information behavior study guided by participatory design methodology; and (b) needs that must be fulfilled in conducting the information behavior study. The needs are triggered by the envisaged purpose and outcomes of the research project which are refined by participants during the course of the project based on mutual learning and idea generation (manifesting in Third Space and involving both individual prior knowledge and the new individual and group learning). From information behavior research, it is clear that there are still many problems in identifying dormant information needs and to work through the different levels on which information needs are often recognized and expressed (Shenton, 2007).

**Envisioning a future outcome such as a new theory, model, recommendation, or information object:** This will relate to the purpose and goal of the research study.

Two phases are identified in Figure 6.2. Phase 1 concerns the *review and stimulation (triggering) and studying of information behavior and information practices* where information behavior activities start during the information behavior researcher's conceptualization of the problem and the planning stages. This entails mostly individual activities such as literature searchers or talking to others but does not exclude collaborative work between a team of researchers. For the use case, this can include scoping reviews from the supporting disciplines, e.g., health information seeking, health communication, cancer prevention and the specific cancer(s). Participants can also create shared databases for references or reach out to experts who might not be part of the team. There would be many iterations in a nonlinear style with strong idiosyncrasies between individual participants. Exactly how Phase 1 will manifest itself in the application of the TSIB study framework is unknown at this stage and requires further research. For now, it is a theoretical framework based on our understanding as set out in preceding chapters. Phase 2 concerns a *hybrid of individual and collaborative interaction*. During both phases, but more specifically during Phase 2, boundary objects are used to stimulate thinking, sharing and facilitating learning. Individual participants and end-users enter this phase with their *individual prior knowledge and experience*. A Xhosa mother may only know about cervical cancer from the experiences of family and friends. She may have limited understanding of the explanation by an English-speaking doctor or oncology nurse on why regular screening is essential (Westbrook and Fourie, 2015). An oncology nurse might come with background and expertise, gained from her research with Xhosa cancer patients (Lourens, 2013).

The participating oncologist and dietician may have mostly experience with cancer prevention campaigns in affluent, urban contexts, while the rural general practitioner (i.e., doctor) may know the people form the Indigenous community, but with limited knowledge of cancer prevention and health communication strategies. The expert in participatory design may have completed many human interface design projects but may have no experience in cross-cultural work with Indigenous communities or South African ethnic traditions and cultures. The language expert may be able to communicate with the end-users in their native language, isiXhosa, but may have no expertise in conducting information behavior studies or in cancer prevention campaigning. Other information behavior experts may have some understanding of rural contexts and although they might speak another of the Indigenous languages—seSotho—they might not be familiar with the Xhosa traditions. In a similar manner, we can speculate on the prior knowledge and experiences of the participants in the design and execution of the information behavior study. The team of participants, including the researchers who initiated the project and the end-users may "move" into a Third Space. This space can take different physical or virtual forms. A physical space may be field trips to the rural areas and dwellings where end-users reside or the local hospital or rooms of a general practitioner in the rural area. The physical form for interaction between participants may include a sangoma—a typical traditional healer. When people from such diverse backgrounds come together, it is to be expected that there will be substantial differences in the intellectual understanding of the disease, preventive strategies, background and ability to communicate—the cognitive spaces of participants. The same would apply to conceptual spaces; this would be more challenging due to language barriers. For a similar study with affluent end-users in a rural or urban area, it would certainly be possible to use virtual spaces such as Zoom meetings to share information and ideas. Gradually participants should move to *individual and collectively gained and learned knowledge*. Information sharing happens through all the phases and applies to all components. When applying a participatory design methodology an essential difference with how information behavior studies is normally conducted, is how the values of participatory design can ensure the freedom, safe space, and encouragement for all participants to have a voice throughout all the steps of an information behavior research project. The Third Space manifests in this contextual space. The different spaces in the Third Space will not be fleshed out in this use case. As noted earlier, the other dimensions also need to be reckoned with, namely: the *temporal, internal and external, and stratified/multilayered dimensions*. In an information behavior study, participants need to work through various levels of complexity. The exact nature of these dimensions needs to be determined by further research when applying the TSIB study framework that we are proposing in Figure 6.2.

### 7.1.2    USE CASE 2: PUBLIC BLENDED SPACE: THE DIGITAL DIARY MEMORY TABLE

As another example, we describe a *digital diary memory table* for information sharing activities such as sharing ideas, memories, and thoughts. In addition, this example also highlights a less considered aspect of information behavior, that of the creation of new information in the form of writing diaries including images and videos. Here we will include some of the above-mentioned elements from our TSIB study framework that can be included in the design of an information behavior study.

**Environment and context:** Let us assume we are in a larger city somewhere in the world. In that city there is a certain place that people can visit occasionally. Such a place could be a museum or a specific event like an exhibition or festival or other places for social and informational interactions, such a public park bench (Čakovská et al. 2019; Zedlacher et al., 2019). In our specific case, the environment is a café in a typical city center. This represents the outer contextual boundary or frame of the setting (cf., Figure 6.2 and 6.3). When entering the café, there are chairs and tables situated in the café. Each of the tables have 2 or 4 chairs. Half of the tables are equipped with a technology (a digital device) that supports different information behavior activities such as searching, browsing, information sharing, but it also supports writing personal information items in the form of a diary. We call this a *digital diary memory table*.

**Participants and information needs:** Visitors (customers) may then come in on a regular basis or occasionally to sit down in the café. In the café, there are other people such as the café owner and two workers serving the customers and one person working in the kitchen. Sometimes, there need to be things fixed in the café such as the lighting or reworking some furniture and thus the café is also visited by professional workers occasionally. Finally, even more rarely, other visitors may enter like a policeman. From a participatory perspective, all these people are important to consider if we want to study information behavior processes as well as their roles and information need situations. All people involved may be considered as end-users of the digital diary table as shown in Figures 6.1, 6.3, and 6.4. Furthermore, they all have different goals with their activities within the café. Their intentions to visit the café are different and their "planned" activities are to satisfy those intentions. In addition to going to the café to do the "normal" things like drinking, eating, and having a chat with friends or family, this situation involves that the different stakeholders and end-users (i.e., participants) have different (user) needs and requirements regarding their tasks (cf., Figure 6.2). From a TSIB study point of view, it is necessary to listen to and consider all involved end-users and stakeholders in order to understand their information behavior processes and activities. So, from the perspective of the manager of the café, it is very important that the manager understand what function this digital memory table will play. To reach this understanding, a study needs to include customers and other visitors and their viewpoints. From the manager's point of view and the regular customers point of view, they may have a diverting or common goal, and the goal may be contradicted by occasional visitors and other aspects, such as laws and regulations. All these things need to be discussed and may be studied using the TSIB study framework which focuses on considering all involved people's information goals, intentions and information needs. This is most important in order to (a) study the individual and collaborative and intersectional information behavior processes as well as (b) when the goal is to develop or enhance the technology-based digital memory table and its functions.

**Information activities:** As mentioned, the owner or manager of the café has introduced and installed (or want to install) a *digital memory table* that allows visitors and others to perform different informational activities such as write and draw on a digital surface using some tool (it could be a physical pen on a digital surface or an Augmented Reality application). When the café customers sit down, they may, either individually or in a group, interact with the digital diary memory table as well as interact with each other through the device. The design idea with the memory table is that people will write on the table in a diary form (cf., Figure 6.6), thus creating new information. The information contributed in this form may be written in very different styles, lengths and forms. It could be announcements of personal situations like "Today I am getting married!" It may also be in a more poetic form or personal reflections expressing empathy or frustration. The person writing these items may take part of other people's information or write with the intention that it might be shared. If the person visits on a regular basis, urban "stories" may be emerging. Stories that a specific person continues to write on or it could be a collaborative effort. The information may also be small comments on life, actual emotions and feelings. Furthermore, the visitors may bring in information to the café/digital memory table from outside and they may also leave the café/memory table with information. This could be utilized by extending the digital memory table with a mobile application that connects to the table and thus constitutes a blended space. From a security and privacy point of view, it may not be possible to insert comments on others' input. The activities could be done together with friends sitting at the table at the same time (synchronously) or if you are alone, you can share and/or add your own small stories (asynchronously) (cf., Figure 6.5). Using our TSIB study framework will consider all end-users and different types of information activities involved during a short time period or through a longitudinal study.

**Boundary zones and objects and intersectional zones:** The technology (the digital memory diary table) that is embedded into the café table will act as a boundary object (cf., Figures 6.1a, and 6.1b, 6.3, and 6.6 in particular). The goal with the memory table is to create a shared space for the customers (and perhaps also the other stakeholders). The envisioned goal with that, is to offer the customers the opportunity to create and generate an information object that can be shared with other known or unknown customers. This table with the digital surface populated with people sharing their everyday experiences and knowledge is done in a Third Space.

Through the technology, end-users take part in an individual and/or collaborative activity. The information activities may be connected to highly personal comments and opinions to include links and comments on regional, national and international events and activities. The digital memory table with its physical and digital blended spaces initiates and triggers actions and information sharing, but also, through its boundaries, it formulates the creation of an information object(s) that emerge as an outcome of joint activities. The devices (the memory table) also have their strengths and weaknesses and those can be studied using the TSIB study framework.

For example, if we want to develop studies that focus on how information objects may be created or if the focus is on how to develop the device, the application of the TSIB study framework and its suggested concepts of boundary zones, we may frame variables to be considered. Furthermore, using the concepts of intersectional zones, we may study how people and devices interact and how they affect each other. From a design point of view, manipulating or reshaping the boundary object (the digital diary table) we may study changing information activities and information behavior processes.

The outcome (cf., Figure 6.6) will be a "story" telling of time and synthesized, filtered, assembled and structured, perhaps by the café owner or the writer or a third party, and it might be developed into a book of poems, a book of emotions, comments made on real-life events (cf., Figure 6.6), in digital or physical form. Or it may just be fragments or time-stamps that can be browsed through and as such a new intention or habit to visit the café may have been created, which in turn can be developed into a certain time-related community activity, for example, activities related to climate change. The creation of information objects and information activities can be studied applying information behavior methods as well as the lens of participation of how these information objects are created and used. Thus, within the Third Space that has been created, we might study, as Buckland (1991) has pointed out, information as a process, information as an object and information as knowledge. Furthermore, since different types of end-users are dealing with the creation of this information object, we can study information interaction processes.

Using our TSIB study framework (cf., Figure 6.2, 6.3), this topic can be studied in different ways applying for example a spatial approach, e.g., studying the physical place and device in the café in the city center and its related information behavior processes or in a virtual distributed information space or how the technologies are used or how they may be developed. A temporal dimension, that is, the creation, sharing and "story-telling" could be observed across specific topics or different users within shorter or more longitudinal time-periods. In both cases, different participatory techniques and methods for collecting and analyzing data may be used. The stratified dimension reflects that the context can be studied using the TSIB study framework and its stratified dimensions, different layers, and levels of engagements and information need complexities, can be investigated. Finally, the development, evolution, and creation of the "stories" as well as of the technology device, may be observed.

## 7.2   WAY FORWARD

Information handling activities and specifically information sharing, may be used more explicitly as important elements and processes when different design activities are planned and executed. Very seldom information activities other than information seeking and searching have been a specific focus in design processes when developing user interfaces for information systems. Our framework embraces information activities (such as the sharing of information) as a vital part of any design process, both within the information behavior research area as well as within the HCI area either utilizing participatory design or other methodologies. It can also be applied in many other contexts like information activities, in which information sharing and creative and interaction design processes are intertwined, and for which we need a growing understanding of their mutual dependencies and symbiotic relationships.

We need to better understand how information objects are generated and created, developed, utilized, and envisioned in future applications, systems, services and artefacts embedded in a diversity and complexity of people, contexts and domains. We also need to conduct information behavior studies that bring us closer to information related solutions that can address the complexities of users' information needs and the many information related challenges faced in contemporary society. Participation and participatory design are an approach that can move us forward exploring spaces and places for information interaction and in identifying appropriate theories from interdisciplinary perspectives.

# Appendix A: General Guideline for Conducting a Participatory Design Workshop Called Future Workshop

## PARTICIPATORY DESIGN WORKSHOP

A participatory design workshop is one in which users, designers, researchers, and stakeholders/end-users work together to design alternative ideas for a certain problem. Participatory design is about the direct involvement of people in the co-design of the technologies they use. Its main focus is on how people-driven collaborative design processes can unfold the technologies that will be used by these same people. Essentially, participatory design is the practice of participation.

**Preparing for a participatory design workshop (not in any specific order)**

- Acquire knowledge of the problem domain.

- Prepare at least one possible idea (without exposing it during workshop since each of the participants need to contribute with at least one individual idea and not adapt to another participant).

- Prepare scenarios or stories.

- Create an agenda for the workshop.

- Decide on roles for the participants.

- Develop techniques to be used (and back-up).

- Book a space.

- Prepare material that has been decided to be used.

## When is a participatory design workshop appropriate?

Participatory design workshops are most effective early in the design process. Ideas and reasoning are in an early stage for both the users and the designers and are exposed to minimal limitations.

## Participatory design Future Workshop may contain:

1. Preparation

    a. Inform yourself as a designer

    b. Workplace visit

2. Critique phase

3. Envisioning phase

4. Implementation phase

5. Follow-up

## Who should attend?

Generally, but not exclusively, a participatory design workshop should involve 8–10 people:

- At least between 2–6 representative expert users from the target domain. Their knowledge and value could not be overestimated

- A business and or management representative or system administrator when applicable

- A developer/programmer

- A facilitator/moderator from the research team

- A person responsible for data collection from the research team

## Roles in the design process (for example)

- Stakeholder (e.g., members of the company/organization for which a certain system, service, or tool is being designed)

- Participants and end-users (representatives of the intended users)

- Developer (programmer of a future service, etc.)

- Facilitator and generator (persons that leads the design workshop together with participants and stakeholders)

- Researcher (could have several roles like facilitator and designer)

- Designer (the designer and researcher may be the same person)

**Participants roles (for example)**

- Working as an information source

- Working as a co-designer

- Working as a reviewer

**Three modes of participation**

- Community participation

  ○ People world (concrete space)

- Public participation

  ○ Experts world (abstract world)

- Design participation

# Bibliography

Abbass-Dick, J., Brolly, M., Huizinga, J., Newport, A., Xie, F.L., George, S. and Sterken, E. (2018). Designing an eHealth breastfeeding resource with indigenous families using a participatory design. *Journal of Transcultural Nursing*, 29(5), 480–488. DOI: 10.1177/1043659617731818. 48, 56

Agarwal, N. (2018). *Exploring Context in Information Behavior: Seeker, Situation, Surroundings, and Shared Identities*. Morgan & Claypool Publishers. DOI: 10.1002/asi.24102. 51

Akoglu, C. and Dankl, K. (2019). Co-creation for empathy and mutual learning: a framework for design in health and social care. *CoDesign*. DOI: 10.1080/15710882.2019.1633358. 23

Alfer, A. (2017). Entering the translab: translation as collaboration, collaboration as translation, and the third space of "translaboration". *Translation and Translanguaging in Multilingual Contexts*, 3(3), 275–290. DOI: 10.1075/ttmc.3.3.01alf. 35

Allin, S., Shepherd, J., Tomasone, J., Munce, S., Linassi, G., Hossain, S. N. and Jaglal, S. (2018). Participatory design of an online self-management tool for users with spinal cord injury: qualitative study. *JMIR Rehabilitation and Assistive Technologies*, 5(1), 1. DOI: 10.2196/rehab.8158. xxi, 58, 59

Amoamo, M. (2011). Tourism and hybridity: re-visiting Bhabha's third space. *Annals of Tourism Research*, 38(4), 1254–1273. DOI: 10.1016/j.annals.2011.04.002. 35

Apel, H. (2004). The Future Workshop. Deutsches Institut für Erwachsenenbildung, März 2004. http://www.die-bonn.de/esprid/dokumente/doc-2004/apel04_02.pdf. 27

Attfield, S., Blandford, A., and Makri, S. (2010). Social and interactional practices for disseminating current awareness information in an organisational setting. *Information Processing and Management*, 46(6), 632–645. DOI: 10.1016/j.imp.2009.10.003. 61

Awan, W. A., Ameen, K., and Soroya, S.H. (2019). Information encountering and sharing behavior of research students in an online environment. *Aslib Journal of Information Management*, 71(4), 500–517. DOI: 10.1108/ajim-10-2018-0232. 61

Aytekin, B. A. and Rızvanoğlu, K. (2019). Creating learning bridges through participatory design and technology to achieve sustainability in local crafts: a participatory model to enable the transfer of tacit knowledge and experience between the traditional craftsmanship and academic education. *International Journal of Technology and Design Education*, 29(3), 603–632. DOI: 10.1007/s10798-018-9454-3. xxi

Ayub, Y. I. R., Kogeda, O. P., and Lall, M. (2018). Capturing tacit knowledge: a case of traditional doctors in Mozambique. *South African Journal of Information Management*, 20(1), a880. DOI: 10.4102/sajim.v20i1.880. 57

Ballantyne, N., Wong, Y. C., and Morgan, G. (2017). Human services and the fourth industrial revolution: from husITa 1987 to husITa 2016. *Journal of Technology in Human Services*, 35(1), 1–7. DOI: 10.1080/15228835.2017.1277900. 2

Bang, M. and Vossoughi, S. (2016). Participatory design research and educational justice: studying learning and relations within social change making. *Cognition and Instruction*, 34(3), 173–193. DOI: 10.1080/07370008.2016.1181879. 61

Bao, X. and Bouthillier, F. (2007). Information sharing: as a type of information behavior. In *Proceedings of the 35th Annual Conference of the Canadian Association for Information Science*, McGill University, Montreal, May 10–12, 2007 (pp.1–14). DOI: 10.29173/cais198. 47, 50

Barcellini, F., Prost, L., and Cerf, M. (2015). Designers' and users' roles in participatory design: what is actually co-designed by participants? *Applied Ergonomics*, 50, 31–40. DOI: 10.1016/j. apergo.2015.02.005. 4, 27, 56, 58

Belkin, N. J. (1980). Anomalous states of knowledge as a basis for information retrieval. *Canadian Journal of Information Science*, 5(1), 133–143. 52

Bell, K. E., Orbe, M. P., Drummond, D. K., and Camara, S. K. (2000). Accepting the challenge of centralizing without essentializing: black feminist thought and African American women's communicative experiences. *Women's Studies in Communication*, 23(1), 41–62. DOI: 10.1080/07491409.2000.11517689. 60

Belluzzo, R. C. B. and Rosetto, M. (2021). 21st century skills and competences: challenges with a focus in information and communication. In E. da Silva and M.L.P. Valentim (Eds.), *Role of Information Science in a Complex Society* (pp. 1–16). IGI Global. DOI: 10.4018/978-1-7998-6512-4.ch001. 1

Benyon, D. (2014). Spaces of interaction, places for experience. In J.M. Carroll (Ed.) *Synthesis Lectures on Human-Centered Information*. Morgan & Claypool Publishers. DOI: 10.2200/S00595ED1V01Y201409HCI022. 49

Bergold, J. and Thomas, S. (2012). Participatory research methods: a methodological approach in motion. *Historical Social Research/Historische Sozialforschung*, 13(1), 191–222. 57

Bessant, C. (Ed.). (2009). *Information Sharing Handbook*. The Law Society. xxi, 49

Bhabha, H. K. (1994). *The Location of Culture*. Routledge. 34, 35, 42

Bhabha, H. K. (1990). *Nation and Narration*. Routledge. 34

Blake, C. and Pratt, W. (2006a). Collaborative information synthesis I: a model of information behaviors of scientists in medicine and public health. *Journal of the American Society for Information Science and Technology*, 57(13), 1740–1749. DOI: 10.1002/asi.20487. 53

Blake, C. and Pratt, W. (2006b). Collaborative information synthesis II: recommendations for information systems to support synthesis activities. *Journal of the American Society for Information Science and Technology*, 57(14), 1888–1895. DOI: 10.1002/asi.20486. 53

Bødker, S (2006). When second wave HCI meets third wave challenges. In *NordiCHI '06: Proceedings of the 4th Nordic Conference on Human–Computer Interaction* (pp. 1–8). ACM Digital Library. DOI: 10.1145/1182475.1182476. 19

Bødker, S. and Iversen, O. S. (2002). Staging a professional participatory design practice: moving PD beyond the initial fascination of user involvement. In *Proceedings of the Second Nordic Conference on Human–Computer Interaction* (pp. 11–18). ACM Digital Library. DOI: 10.1145/572020.572023. 62

Bødker, S. and Kyng, M. (2018). Participatory design that matters—facing the big issues. *ACM Transactions on Computer-Human Interaction*, 25(1), Article 4. DOI: 10.1145/3152421. 32

Bonito, J. A. (2007). A local model of information sharing in small groups. *Communication Theory*, 17(3), 252–280. DOI: 10.1111/j.1468-2885.2007.00295. 57, 62

Brandt, E., Binder, T., and Sanders, E. B-N. (2012). Tools and techniques: ways to engage telling, making and enacting. In J. Simonsen and T. Robertson (Eds.), *Routledge International Handbook of Participatory Design* (pp.145–181). Routledge. DOI: 10.4324/9780203108543.ch7. 22, 25

Bratteteig, T. and Wagner, I. (2016). Unpacking the notion of participation in participatory design. *Computer Supported Cooperative Work (CSCW)* 25, 425–475. DOI 10.1007/s10606-016-9259-4. 20, 21

Bratteteig, T. and Wagner, I. (2012). Disentangling power and decision-making in participatory design. In *PDC2012.Proceedings of the 12th Participatory Design Conference. Research. Papers*, vol. 1. 2012 ACM, pp. 41–50. DOI: 10.1145/2347635.2347642. 22

Buchmüller, S., Joost, G., Bessing, N., and Stein, S. (2011). Bridging the gender and generation gap by ICT applying a participatory design process. *Personal and Ubiquitous Computing*, 15(7), 743–758. DOI: 10.1007/s00779-011-0388-y. xxi

Buckland, M. K. (1991). Information as thing. *Journal of the American Society for Information Science*, 42(5), 351–360. DOI: 10.1002/(SICI)1097-4571(199106)42. 9, 15, 79, 93

Bukhari, S., Hamid, S., and Ravana, S. D. (2016). Merging the models of information seeking behavior to generate the generic phases. In *Proceedings of the 3rd International Conference on Information Retrieval and Knowledge Management (CAMP)* (pp. 125–130). IEEE. DOI: 10.1109/INFRKM.2016.7806348. 51

Byrne, E. and Sahay, S. (2007). Participatory design for social development: a South African case study on community-based health information systems. *Information Technology for Development*, 13(1), 71–94. DOI: 10.1002/itdj.20052. 56, 57

Byström, K. and Hansen, P. (2005). Conceptual framework for tasks in information studies. *Journal of the American Society for Information Science and Technology*, 56(10), 1050–1061. DOI: 10.1002/asi.20197. 58

Čakovská, B., Bihuňová, M., Hansen, P., Marcheggiani, E., and Galli A. (2019). Methodological approaches to reflect on the relationships between people, spaces, technologies. In C.S. Costa, I.Š. Erjavec, T. Kenna, M. de Lange, K. Ioannidis, G. Maksymiuk, and M. de Waal (Eds.), *CyberParks – The Interface Between People, Places and Technology* (pp. 251–261). Springer. (Lecture Notes in Computer Science, 11380). DOI: 10.1007/978-3-030-13417-4_20. 91

Calderon, R. (2016). Third-placeness: Supporting the Experience of Third Place with Interactive Public Displays. (University of British Columbia Ph.D. dissertation) DOI: 10.14288/1.0307293. 43, 44

Case, D. O. and Given, L. M. (Eds.). (2016). *Looking for Information: a Survey of Research on Information Seeking, Needs, and Behavior*. Emerald Group Publishing Limited. DOI: 10.1108/S2055-53772016. 5, 51, 58, 66, 76, 77

Chow, C. W., Harrison, G. L., McKinnon, J. L., and Wu, A. (1999). Cultural influences on informal information sharing in Chinese and Anglo-American organizations: an exploratory study. *Accounting Organizations and Society*, 24(7), 561–582. DOI: 10.1016/S0361-3682(99)00022-7. 57, 59

Clack, L., Stühlinger, M., Meier, M-T., Wolfensberger, A., and Sax, H. (2019). User-centred participatory design of visual cues for isolation precautions. *Antimicrobial Resistance and Infection Control*, 8(1), 179. DOI: 10.1186/s13756-019-0629-9. 48

Cochran, P. A., Marshall, C. A., Garcia-Downing, C., Kendall, E., Cook, D., McCubbin, L., and Gover, R. M. (2008). Indigenous ways of knowing: implications for participatory research and community. *American Journal of Public Health*, 98(1), 22–27. DOI: 10.2105/AJPH.2006.093641. 47

Cole, C. (2012). *Information Need: a Theory Connecting Information to Knowledge Formation*. Information Today, Inc. 52

Collins, N., Chou, Y-M., Warner, M., and Rowley, C. (2017). Human factors in East Asian virtual teamwork: a comparative study of Indonesia, Taiwan and Vietnam. *International Journal of Human Resource Management*, 28(10), 1475–1498. DOI: 10.1080/09585192.2015.1089064. 58, 60

Conole, G., Scanlon, E., Littleton, K., Kerawalla, L., and Mulholland, P. (2010). Personal inquiry: innovations in participatory design and models for inquiry learning. *Educational Media International*, 47(4), 277–292. DOI: 10.1080/09523987.2010.535328. 61, 63

Cook, M. (2005). A place of their own: creating a classroom "third space" to support a continuum of text construction between home and school. *Literacy*, 39(2), 85–90. DOI: 10.1111/j.1741-4350.2005.00405.x. 39

Conley Tyler, M. H., Bretherton, D., Halafoff, A., and Nietschke, Y. (2008). Developing a peace education curriculum for Vietnamese primary schools: a case study of participatory action research in cross-cultural design. *Journal of Research in International Education*, 7(3), 346–368. DOI: 10.1177/1475240908096487. 48

Corrado, A. M., Benjamin-Thomas, T. E., McGrath, C., Hand, C., and Rudman, D. L. (2020). Participatory action research with older adults: a critical interpretive synthesis. *Gerontologist*, 60(5), E413–E427. DOI: 10.1093/geront/gnz080. 56

Dalsgaard, P. (2010). Challenges of participation in large-scale public projects. In *Proceedings of the 11th Biennial Participatory Design Conference on - PDC'10* (pp. 21–30). ACM Digital Library. DOI: 10.1145/1900441.1900445. 12

Danielsson, K. and Wiberg, C. (2006). Participatory design of learning media: designing educational computer games with and for teenagers. *Interactive Technology and Smart Education*, 3(4), 275–291. DOI: 10.1108/17415650680000068. 58

De Koning, J. I. J. C., Crul, M., and Wever, R. (2016). Models of co-creation. In N. Morelli, A. de Götzen, and F. Grani (Eds.), *Proceedings of the 5th Service Design and Innovation Conference: ServDes. 2016* (pp. 266–278). Linköping University Electronic Press. 30, 31

Demetriades, S. Z. and Walter, N. (2016). You should know better: can self-affirmation facilitate information-seeking behavior and interpersonal discussion? *Journal of Health Communication*, 21(11), 1131–1140. DOI: 10.1080/10810730.2016.1224280. 61

Dervin, B. (1993). From the mind's eye of the user: the sense-making qualitative methodology. In J. D. Glazier and R. R. Powell (Eds.), *Qualitative Research in Information Management* (pp. 61–84). Libraries Unlimited. 52

Dervin, B. and Foreman-Wernet, L. (with E. Lauterbach). (2003). *Sense-Making Methodology Reader: Selected Writings from Brenda Dervin*. Hampton Press. 55

Design Council. (2015). *Design Methods Step 1-4*. https://www.designcouncil.org.uk/news-opinion/design-methods-step-1-discover (Archived by the Internet Archive at https://web.archive.org/web/20201029175747/https://www.designcouncil.org.uk/news-opinion/design-methods-step-1-discover). 30

Devine, D. J. (1999). Effects of cognitive ability, task knowledge, information sharing, and conflict on group decision-making effectiveness. *Small Group Research*, 30(5), 608–634. DOI: 10.1177/104649649903000506. 57, 62

Dimopoulos-Bick, T., Dawda, P., Maher, L., and Palmer, V. (2018). Experience-based co-design: tackling common challenges. *The Journal of Health Design*, 3(1), 86–93. DOI: 10.21853/JHD.2018.46. 23

DiSalvo, B., Yip, J., Bonsignore, E., and DiSalvo, C. (2017). Participatory design for learning. In B. DiSalvo, J. Yip, E. Bonsignore and C. DiSalvo (Eds.), *Participatory Design for Learning: Perspectives from Practice and Research* (pp. 16–21). Routledge. DOI: 10.4324/9781315630830. xxi, xxii, 55

Dittrich, Y. and Lindeberg, O. (2004). How use-oriented development can take place. *Information and Software Technology*, 46(9), 603–617. DOI: 10.1016/j.infsof.2003.11.002. 23

D'Souza, N. S. (2006). *Design Intelligences: A Case for Multiple Intelligences in Architectural Design*. Ann Arbor, The University of Wisconsin–Milwaukee. 60

Duckles, J. and Moses, G. (2018). Aligning collaborative and transformative research with local ways of knowing and being. *International Journal of Qualitative Methods*, 17(1), 11. 48, 59

Du, J. T. (2014). The information journey of marketing professionals: incorporating work task-driven information seeking, information judgments, information use, and information sharing. *Journal of the Association for Information Science and Technology*, 65(9), 1850–1869. DOI: 10.1002/asi.23085. 52

Du, J. T., Mohammad Arif, A. S. and Hansen, P. (2019). Collaborative query reformulation in tourism information search, *Online Information Review*, 43(7), 1115–1135. DOI: 10.1108/OIR-12-2018-0371. 11

Dunne, J. E. (2002). Information seeking and use by battered women: a 'person-in-progressive-situations' approach. *Library and Information Science Research*, 24(4), 343–355. (https://search-proquest-com.uplib.idm.oclc.org/docview/57569157?accountid=14717) DOI: 10.1016/S0740-8188(02)00132-9. 54

Eckerdal, J. R. (2012). Information sources at play: The apparatus of knowledge production in contraceptive counselling. *Journal of Documentation*, 68(3), 278–298. DOI: 10.1108/00220411211225548. 14

Egilsdottir, H. Ö., Heyn, L. G., Brembo, E. A., Byermoen, K. R., Moen, A., and Eide, H. (2021). Configuration of mobile learning tools to support basic physical assessment in nursing education: longitudinal participatory design approach. *JMIR mHealth and uHealth*, 9(1), e22633. DOI: 10.2196/22633. 1, 2

Ehn, P. (2008). Participation in design things. In *Proceedings of the 10th Anniversary Conference on Participatory Design* (pp. 92–101). ACM Digital Library. 30

Ehn, P. (1993). Scandinavian design: on participation and skill. In D. Schuler and A. Namioka (Eds.), Participatory Design: Principles and Practices (pp.41–87). Lawrence Erlbaum. DOI: 10.1201/9780203744338-4. 21

Ehn, P. (1989). *Work-oriented Design of Computer Artifacts*. Lawrence Erlbaum. 12

Ehn, P. and Kyng, M. (1987). The collective resources approach to systems design. In G. Bjerknes, P. Ehn, and M. Kyng (Eds.), *Computers and Democracy—a Scandinavian Challenge* (pp. 17–58). Gower Publishing. 19

Eisenberg, J. and Mattarelli, E. (2017). Building bridges in global virtual teams: the role of multicultural brokers in overcoming the negative effects of identity threats on knowledge sharing across subgroups. *Journal of International Management*, 23(4), 399–411. DOI: 10.1016/j.intman.2016.11.007. 60

Ellis, D. (1989). A behavioral approach to information retrieval design. *Journal of Documentation*, 45(3), 171–212. DOI: 10.1108/eb026843. 48, 52, 61

Elmborg, J., Jacobs, H. L., McElroy, K., and Nelson, R. L. (2015). Making a third space for student voices in two academic libraries. *Reference and User Services Quarterly*, 55(2), 144. DOI: 10.5860/rusq.55n2.144. 39

Elmborg, J. K. (2011). Libraries as the spaces between us: recognizing and valuing the third space. *Reference and User Services Quarterly*, 50(4), 338–350. DOI: 10.5860/rusq.50n4.338. 39

Erdelez, S. (2004). Investigation of information encountering in the controlled research environment. *Information Processing and Management*, 40(6), 1013–1025. DOI: 10.1016/j.ipm.2004.02.002. 61

Erdelez, S. (1999). Information encountering: it's more than just bumping into information. *Bulletin of the American Society for Information Science and Technology*, 25(3), 26–29. DOI: 10.1002/bult.118. 61

Erdelez, S. and Rioux, K. (2000). Sharing information encountered for others on the Web. *The New Review of Information Behaviour: Studies in Information Seeking in Context*, 1, 219–233. 52

Eriksson, S. and Hansen, P. (2017). HeartBeats—a speculative proposal for ritualization of digital objects. In *Proceedings of the 2017 ACM Conference Companion Publication on Designing Interactive Systems* (pp. 218–222). ACM Digital Library. DOI: 10.1145/3064857.3079149. 49

Faiola, A. (2007). The design enterprise: rethinking the HCI education paradigm. *Design Issues*, 23(3), 30-45. DOI: 10.1162/desi.2007.23.3.30. 55

Falconer, J. (2014). *Photovoice Participatory-Action Research Design and Adaptations for Adverse Fieldwork Conditions*. SAGE Publications Ltd. DOI: 10.4135/9781446273050135192233. xxi

Fanderclai, T. (1996). Like magic, only real. In L. Cherny and E.R. Weise (Eds.), *Wired Women: Gender and New Realities in Cyberspace*. Seal Press. 40

Fang, J. and Strobel, J. (2011). How ID models help with game-based learning: an examination of the gentry model in a participatory design project. *Educational Media International*, 48(4), 287-306. DOI: 10.1080/09523987.2011.632277. 49

Fardous, J., Du, J. T., Choo, K-K. R., Huang, S., and Hansen, P. (2017). Exploring collaborative information search behavior of mobile social media users in trip planning. In *Proceedings of the iConference 2017* (pp. 435-444). iSchools. DOI: 10.1145/3020165.3022167. 11

Fidel, R. (2012). *Human Information Interaction: An Ecological Approach to Information Behavior*. The MIT Press. DOI: 10.7551/mitpress/9780262017008.001.0001. xxiii, 14

Fidel, R. and Pejtersen, A. M. (2004). From information behavior research to the design of information systems: the cognitive work analysis framework. *Information Research*, 10(1), paper 210. http://Informationr.net/ir/10-1/paper210.html (Archived by the Internet Archive at https://web.archive.org/web/20191124174440/http://informationr.net/ir/10-1/paper210.html). 51

Fisher, K. E., Durrance, J. C. and Hinton, M. B. (2004). Information grounds and the use of need-based services by immigrants in Queens, New York: a context-based, outcome evaluation approach. *Journal of the American Society for Information Science and Technology*, 55(8), 754–766. DOI: 10.1002/asi.20019. 61

Fisher, K .E., Bishop, A. P., Magassa, L. and Fawcett, P. (2014a). Action! Co-designing interactive technology with immigrant teens. *IDC'14: Proceedings of the 2014 Conference on Interaction Design and Children* (pp. 345–348). ACM Digital Library. DOI: 10.1145/2593968.2610488. 61

Fisher, K. E., Bishop, A. P., Fawcett, P. and Magassa, L. (2014b). InfoMe: a field-design methodology for research on ethnic minority youth as information mediaries. *New Directions in Children's and Adolescents' Information Behavior Research* (Library and Information Science, Vol. 10) (pp. 135–156). Emerald Group Publishing Limited. DOI: 10.1108/S1876-056220140000010053. 61

Fisher, K. E., Erdelez, S., and McKechnie, L. (2006). *Theories of Information Behavior*. American Society for Information Science and Technology. 49, 73

Fisher, K. E., Landry, C. F. and Naumer, C. (2007). Social spaces, casual interactions, meaningful exchanges: "information ground" characteristics based on the college student experience. *Information Research*, 12(2), paper 291. http://informationr.net/ir/12-2/paper291.html (Archived by the Internet Archive at https://web.archive.org/web/20201124185558/http://informationr.net/ir/12-2/paper291.html), 35

Fisher, K., Naumer, C., Durrance, J., Stromski, L. and Christiansen, T. (2005). Something old, something new: preliminary findings from an exploratory study about people's information habits and information grounds. *Information Research*, 10(2), paper 223. http://informationr.net/ir/10-2/paper223.html (Archived by the Internet Archive at https://web.archive.org/web/20201125060244/http://informationr.net/ir/10-2/paper223.html). 35

Fisher, K. E., Dresang, E., Davis, K., Fawcett, P., Bishop, A. and Magassa, L. (2013). Teen design days: promoting youth civic engagement through design thinking. *Digital Media & Learning Conference*, Chicago, IL. http://dml2013.dmlhub.net/. DOI: 10.1145/2517899.2517914. 61

FitzGerald, L. and Garrison, K. L. (2016). Investigating the guided inquiry process. In S. Kurbanoğlu, J. Boustany, S. Špiranec, E. Grassian, D. Mizrachi, L. Roy and T. Çakmak (Eds.), *Information Literacy: Key to an Inclusive Society* (pp. 667–677). (Communications in Computer and Information Science, vol. 676). Springer. DOI: 10.1007/978-3-319-52162-6_65. 37

Ford, N. (2015). *Introduction to Information Behavior*. Facet Publishing. DOI: 10.29085/9781783301843. 51

Foster, A. (2004). A nonlinear model of information-seeking behavior. *Journal of the American Society for Information Science and Technology*, 55(3), 228–237. DOI: 10.1002/asi.10359. 52

Foster, J. (2006). Collaborative information seeking and retrieval. *Annual Review of Information Science and Technology*, 40, 329–356. DOI: 10.1002/aris.1440400115. 10

Foster, V. (2007). 'Ways of knowing and showing': imagination and representation in feminist participatory social research. *Journal of Social Work Practice*, 21(3), 361–376. DOI: 10.1080/02650530701553732. 48, 55, 59

Fourie, I. (2008). Information needs and information behavior of patients and family members in a cancer palliative care setting: an exploratory study of an existential context from different perspectives. *Information Research*, 13(4), paper 360. http://InformationR.net/ir/13-4/paper360.html (Archived by the Internet Archive at https://web.archive.org/web/20190810140556/http://www.informationr.net/ir//13-4/paper360.html). 87

Fourie, I. and Julien, H. (2014). Ending the dance: a research agenda for affect and emotion in studies of information behavior. *Information Research*, 19(4), 108–124 http://informationr.net/ir/19-4/isic/isic09.html. 88

Fowles, R. A. (2000). Symmetry in design participation in the built environment: experiences and insights from education and practice. In S. A. R. Scrivener, L. J. Ball, and A. Woodcock (Eds.), *Collaborative Design* (pp. 59–70). Springer. DOI: 10.1007/978-1-4471-0779-8_6. 7, 40

Freeman, S., Marston, H. R., Olynick, J., Musselwhite, C., Kulczycki, C., Genoe, R., and Xiong, B. (2020). Intergenerational effects on the impacts of technology use in later life: insights from an international, multi-site study. *International Journal of Environmental Research and Public Health*, 17(16), 5711. DOI: 10.3390/ijerph17165711. 3

Freund, L. and Toms, E. G. (2016). Interacting with archival finding aids. *Journal of the Association for Information Science and Technology*, 67(4), 994–1008. DOI: 10.1002/asi.23436. 14

Friedman, B. and Hendry, D. G. (2019). *Value Sensitive Design: Shaping Technology with Moral Imagination*. The MIT Press. DOI: 10.7551/mitpress/7585.001.0001. 6

Friedman, F. and Nissenbaum, H. (1996). Bias in computer systems. *ACM Transactions on Information Systems (TOIS)*, 14(3), 330-347. DOI: 10.1145/230538.230561.

Gardner, H. E. (1983). *Frames of Mind: The Theory of Multiple Intelligences*. Basic Books. 60

Ginige, A., Paolino, L., Romano, M., Sebillo, M., Tortora, G., and Vitiello, G. (2014). Information sharing among disaster responders—an interactive spreadsheet-based collaboration approach. *Computer Supported Cooperative Work (CSCW)*, 23(4–6), 547–583. DOI: 10.1007/s10606-014-9207-0. 47, 49, 56

Giroux, H. A. (2006). Border pedagogy in the age of postmodernism. In H.A. Giroux (Ed.), *The Giroux Reader* (pp. 47–68). Paradigm Publishers. 42

Given, L. M., Kelly, W., and Willson, R. (2015). Bracing for impact: the role of information science in supporting societal research impact. *Proceedings of the Association for Information Science and Technology*, 52(1), 1–10. DOI: 10.1002/pra2.2015.145052010048.

Godbold, N. (2013). An information need for emotional cues: unpacking the role of emotions in sense making. *Information Research*, 18(1), paper 561. http://informationr.net/ir/18-1/paper561.html#.XxVFBkl7nIU (Archived by the Internet Archive at https://web.archive.org/web/20200719081111/http://informationr.net/ir/18-1/paper561.html#.XxVF60l7nIU). 52

Godbold, N. (2006). Beyond information seeking: towards a general model of information behavior. *Information Research*, 11(4), paper 269. http://informationr.net/ir/11-4/paper269 (Archived by the Internet Archive at https://web.archive.org/web/20190809054528/http://www.informationr.net/ir/11-4/paper269). 52

Godjo, T., Boujut, J. F., Marouzé, C., and Giroux, F. (2015). A participatory design approach based on the use of scenarios for improving local design methods in developing countries. *HAL Archives-ouvertes*.Fr. https://hal.archives-ouvertes.fr/hal-01206430v2. 55

Greenbaum, J. and Kyng, M. (1991). *Design at Work: Cooperative Design of Computer Systems*. Lawrence Erlbaum. 12

Greifeneder, E. (2014). Trends in information behavior research. In Proceedings of ISIC: The Information Behavior Conference, Leeds, 2–5 September: Part 1. *Information Research*, 19(4), paper isic13. http://InformationR.net/ir/19-4/isic/isic13.html (Archived by the Internet Archive at https://web.archive.org/web/20200801162410if_/http://informationr.net/ir///19-4/isic/isic13.html#.XyWXLtJxeM8). 6

Greifeneder, E., Pontis, S., Blandford, A., Attalla, H., Neal, D., and Schlebbe, K. (2018). Researchers' attitudes towards the use of social networking sites. *Journal of Documentation*, 74(1), 119–136. DOI: 10.1108/JD-04-2017-0051 (Archived by the Internet Archive at http://bit.ly/300RGDZ). DOI: 10.1108/JD-04-2017-0051. 5, 6

Grenersen, G., Kemi, K., and Nilsen, S. (2016). Landscapes as documents. *Journal of Documentation*, 72(6), 1181–1196. DOI: 10.1108/JD-01-2016-0010. 47

Gulliksen, J., Lantz, A., and Boivie, I. (1999). User centered design—problems and possibilities: a summary of the 1998 PDC and CSCW workshop. *ACM SIGCHI Bulletin*, 31(2), 25. DOI: 10.1145/329657.329666. 12, 20, 21

Gutiérrez, K. D. (2008). Developing a sociocritical literacy in the third space. *Reading Research Quarterly*, 43(2), 148–164. DOI: 10.1598/RRQ.43.2.3. 39

Halskov, K. and Hansen, N. B. (2015). The diversity of participatory design research practice at PDC 2002–2012. *International Journal of Human-Computer Studies*, 74, 81-92. DOI: 10.1016/j.ijhcs.2014.09.003. 27

Hansen, P. and Järvelin, K. (2005). Collaborative information retrieval in an information-intensive domain. *Information Processing and Management*, 41(5), 1101–1119. DOI: 10.1016/j.ipm.2004.04.01. 10, 11, 12, 13, 50

Hansen, P., Loizides, F., and Ioannou, A. (2016). Interacting with technology to interact physically: investigating affordances of tabletops to facilitate collaboration for conflicting users. In D. K. W. Chiu, I. Marenzi, U. Nanni, M. Spanio, and M. Temperini (Eds.), *Proceedings of the 15th International Conference on Advances in Web-Based Learning* (pp. 266–270). Springer. (Lecture Notes in Computer Science, 10013). DOI: 10.1007/978-3-319-47440-3_30. 41

Hansen, P. and Rieh, S. Y. (2016). Editorial: recent advances on searching as learning: an introduction to the special issue. *Journal of Information Science*, 42, 3–6. DOI: 10.1177/0165551515614473. 14

Hansen, P., Shah, C., and Klas, C-P. (Eds.). (2015). *Collaborative Information Seeking: Best Practices, New Domains and New Thoughts*. Springer. DOI: 10.1007/978-3-319-18988-8. 13

Hansen, P. and Widén, G. (2017). The embeddedness of collaborative information seeking in information culture. *Journal of Information Science*, 43(4), 554–566. DOI: 10.1177/0165551516651544. 2, 52

Harmansah, Ö. and Shepherd, N. (2012). The location of theory: a discussion with Homi Bhabha. *Archaeologies*, 8(1), 52–54. DOI: 10.1007/s11759-012-9199-7. 39

Harper, R. and Sellen, A. (1995). Collaborative tools and the practicalities of professional work at the international monetary fund. In *Proceedings of the SIGCHI Conference on Human Factors in Computing Systems* (CHI '95). ACM Press/Addison-Wesley Publishing Co., 122–129. DOI:10.1145/223904.223920. 13

Harper, R. (1998). Information that counts: Sociology, ethnography and work at the international monetary fund. *Proceedings of Workshop on Personalised and Social Navigation in Information Space, Roselagens Pârla*. Sweden Swedish Institute of Computer Science. 13

Hasell, J. (1987). Community design and gaming/ simulation: comparison of communications techniques in participatory design sessions. *Simulation and Gaming*, 18(1), 82–115. DOI: 10.1177/0037550087181005. 62

Heinström, J. (2006). Fast surfing for availability or deep diving into quality: motivation and information seeking among middle and high school students. *Information Research*, 11(4), paper 265. http://InformationR.net/ir/11-4/paper265.html. 52

Hepworth, M. (2004). A framework for understanding user requirements for an information service: defining the needs of informal carers. *Journal of the American Society for Information Science & Technology*, 55(8), 695–708. DOI: 10.1002/asi.20015. xxiii

Hepworth, M. (2007). Knowledge of information behaviour and its relevance to the design of people-centred information products and services. *Journal of Documentation*, 63(1), 33–56. DOI: 10.1108/00220410710723876. xxiii

Hepworth, M., Grunewald, P., and Walton, G. (2014). Research and practice: a critical reflection on approaches that underpin research into people's information behavior. *Journal of Documentation*, 70(6), 1039–1053. DOI: 10.1108/JD-02-2014-0040. 51

Hertzum, M. and Hansen, P. (2019). Empirical studies of collaborative information seeking: a review of methodological issues. *Journal of Documentation*, 75(1), 140–163. DOI: 10.1108/JD-05-2018-0072. 49

Hertzum, M. and Pejtersen, A. M. (2000). The information-seeking practices of engineers: Searching for documents as well as for people. *Information Processing and Management*, 36(5), 761–778. DOI: 10.1016/S0306-4573(00)00011-X. 13

Holmström, J. (1995). The power of knowledge and the knowledge of power: on the systems designer as a translator of rationalities. In B. Dahlbom (Ed.), *Proceedings of the 18th Information Systems Research Seminar (IRIS)*. IRIS Association. 40

Houston, R. and Westbrook, L. (2013). Information-based mitigation of intimate partner violence. Journal of the American Society for Information Science and Technology, 64(8), 1694-1706. DOI: 10.1002/asi.22889. 14

Hussain, S., Sanders, E., and Steinert, M. (2012). Participatory design with marginalized people in developing countries: challenges and opportunities experienced in a field study in Cambodia. *International Journal of Design* [Online] 6:2. Available: http://www.ijdesign.org/index.php/IJDesign/article/view/1054/455. 87, 88

Hyldegård, J. (2009). Beyond the search process – exploring group members' information behavior in context. *Information Processing and Management*, 45(1), 142–158. DOI: 10.1016/j.ipm.2008.05.007. 11

Hyldegård, J. (2006). Collaborative information behavior – exploring Kuhlthau's information search process model in a group-based educational setting. *Information Processing and Management*, 42(1), 276–298. DOI: 10.1016/j.ipm.2004.06.013. 11, 53

IDEO. (2009). *Human Centered Design Toolkit*. (2nd ed.). IDEO. 30

Ishida, T. (Ed.). (2012). Participatory design. In Y. Yamauchi (Ed.), *Introduction to Field Informatics: Kyoto University Field Informatics Research Group* (pp. 123–138). Springer. DOI: 10.1007/978-3-642-29006-0_8. 56

Islind, A., Lindroth, T., Lundin, J., and Steineck, G. (2019). Co-designing a digital platform with boundary objects: bringing together heterogeneous users in healthcare. *Health and Technology*, 9. DOI: 10.1007/s12553-019-00332-5. 88

Janiūnienė, E. and Macevičiūtė, E. (2016). Information sharing between doctoral students and supervisors: fixed roles and flexible attitudes. *Information Research*, 21(4), ISIC 1607. http://Informationr.net/ir/21-4/isic/isic1607.html (Archived by the Internet Archive at https://web.archive.org/web/20190811052658/http://www.informationr.net/ir//21-4/isic/isic1607.html). 51

Jank, D. A. (2010). Toward a unifying ontology for human-information interaction. *Canadian Journal of Information and Library Science*, 34(4), 403–432. DOI: 10.1353/ils.2010.0006. 14

Jensen, C. M., Overgaard, S., Wiil, U. K., and Clemensen, J. (2019). Can tele-health support self-care and empowerment? A qualitative study of hip fracture patients' experiences with testing an "App". *SAGE Open Nursing*, 5. DOI: 10.1177/2377960819825752. 8

Jiang, T. T., Guo, Q., Xu, Y. P., and Fu, S. T. (2019). A diary study of information encountering triggered by visual stimuli on micro-blogging services. *Information Processing and Management*, 56(1), 29–42. DOI: 10.1016/j.ipm.2018.08.005. 49

Johnson, J. D. and Case, D. O. (2012). *Health Information Seeking*. Peter Lang. 52

Jones, P. and Nemeth, C. (2005). Cognitive artifacts in complex work. Y. Cai (Ed.), *Ambient Intelligence for Scientific Discovery, LNAI* 3345, pp. 152–183, 2005. DOI: 10.1007/978-3-540-32263-4_8. 16

Jones, L. M., Wright, K. D., Wallace, M. K., and Veinot, T. (2018). "Take an opportunity whenever you get it": information sharing among African-American women with hypertension. *Journal of the Association for Information Science and Technology*, 69(1), 168–171. DOI: 10.1002/asi.23923. 48

Jónsdóttir, S. R., Gísladóttir, K. R., and Guðjónsdóttir, H. (2015). Using self-study to develop a third space for collaborative supervision of master's projects in teacher education. *Studying Teacher Education*, 11(1), 32–48. DOI: 10.1080/17425964.2015.1013026. 35

Julien, H. and Michels, D. (2004). Intra-individual information behavior in daily life. *Information Processing and Management*, 40(3), 547–562. DOI: 10.1016/S0306-4573(02)00093-6. 54

Jungk, R. and Müllert, N. (1987). *Future Workshops: How to Create Desirable Futures*. Institute for Social Inventions. 25, 27, 29

Kang, M., Choo, P., and Watters, C. E. (2015). Design for experiencing: participatory design approach with multidisciplinary perspectives. *Procedia-Social and Behavioral Sciences*, 174, 830–833. DOI: 10.1016/j.sbspro.2015.01.676. xxii, 56, 58

Karunakaran, A., Reddy, M. C., and Spence, P. R. (2013). Toward a model of collaborative information behavior in organizations. *Journal of the American Society for Information Science and Technology*, 64(12), 2437–2451. DOI: 10.1002/asi.22943. 11, 53

Kendall, L. and Dearden, A. (2018). Disentangling participatory ICT design in socioeconomic development. In *Proceedings of the 15th Participatory Design Conference* (pp. 1–12). ACM Digital Library. DOI: 10.1145/3210586.3210596. 1

Kensing, F. and Greenbaum, J. (2012). Heritage: Having a say. In *Routledge International Handbook of Participatory Design* (pp. 21–36). New York: Routledge. 22, 23

Kensing, F. and Madsen, K. H. (1991). Generating visions: future workshops and metaphors. In J. Greenbaum and M. Kyng (Eds.), *Design at Work* (pp. 155–168). Lawrence Erlbaum. DOI: 10.1201/9781003063988-10. 25, 29

Kensing, F., Simonsen, J., and Bødker, K. (1998). MUST: a method for participatory design. *Human–Computer Interaction*, 13(2), 167–198. DOI: 10.1207/s15327051hci1302_3. 23

Keshavarz, H. (2008). Human information behavior and design, development and evaluation of information retrieval systems. *Program*, 42(4), 391–401. DOI: 10.1108/00330330810912070. xxi, 49, 50, 51

Kjeldskov, J. (2014). *Mobile Interactions in Context: A Designerly Way Toward Digital Ecology*. Morgan & Claypool Publishers; 1st edition (Synthesis Lectures on Human-Centered Informatics). DOI: 10.2200/S00584ED1V01Y201406HCI021. 19, 32

Könings, K. D., Seidel, T., and Van Merriënboer, J. J. (2014). Participatory design of learning environments: integrating perspectives of students, teachers, and designers. *Instructional Science*, 42(1), 1–9. DOI: 10.1007/s11251-013-9305-2. 62

Korošak, T. S., Zavratnik, V., Kos, A., and Duh, E. S. (2018). *Report of Participatory Tools, Methods and Techniques*. Faculty of Electrical Engineering, University of Ljubljana. 48

Kosari, M. and Amoori, A. (2018). Thirdspace: the trialectics of the real, virtual and blended spaces. *Journal of Cyberspace Studies*, 2(2), 163–185. 45

Krauss, K. E. M. (2014). A confessional account of the community entry phases of a critical ethnography: doing emancipatory ICT4D work in a deep rural community in South Africa. In *Proceedings of the 7th Annual SIG GlobDev Pre-ICIS Workshop ICT in Global Development* (pp.1–31). AIS eLibrary. http://aisel.aisnet.org/globdev2014/6 (Archived by the Internet Archive at https://web.archive.org/web/20200603221759/https://aisel.aisnet.org/globdev2014/6/). 59, 87, 88

Krzanowski, R. (2020). What is physical information. *Philosophies*, 5(2), Article 10. DOI: 10.3390/philosophies5020010. 15

Kuhlthau, C. C. (2010). Guided inquiry: school libraries in the 21st century. *School Libraries Worldwide*, 16(1), 17–28. 36, 39

Kuhlthau, C. C. (1999). The role of experience in the information search process of an early career information worker: perceptions of uncertainty, complexity, construction, and sources. *Journal of the American Society for Information Science*, 50(5), 399–412. DOI: 10.1002/(SICI)1097-4571(1999). 51

Kuhlthau, C. C. (1991). Inside the search process: information seeking from the user's perspective. *Journal of the American Society for Information Science*, 42(5), 361–371. 36, 52, 61

Kuhlthau, C. C. (1988). Developing a model of the library search process: cognitive and affective aspects. *RQ*, 28(2), 232. 52

Kuhlthau, C. C. (2004). *Seeking Meaning: A Process Approach to Library and Information Services*. 2nd ed. Libraries Unlimited. 36

Kuhlthau, C. C. and Cole, C. (2012). Third space as an information system and services intervention methodology for engaging the user's deepest levels of information need. *Proceedings of the American Society for Information Science and Technology*, 49(1), 1–6. DOI: 10.1002/meet.14504901074. xxii, 16, 33

Kuhlthau, C. C., Maniotes, L. K., and Caspari, A. K. (2015). *Guided Inquiry: Learning in the 21st Century*. (2nd ed.). Libraries Unlimited. xxii, 7, 16, 33, 35, 36, 37, 39, 40

Landauer, R. (1991). Information is physical, *Physics Today*, 44(5), 23–29. DOI: 10.1063/1.881299. 15

Leckie, G. J., Pettigrew, K. E., and Sylvain, C. (1996). Modelling the information-seeking of professionals: a general model derived from research on engineers, health care professionals, and lawyers. *Library Quarterly*, 66(2), 161–193. DOI: 10.1086/602864. 52

Lee, H. R., Šabanović, S., Chang, W. L., Hakken, D., Nagata, S., Piatt, J., and Bennett, C. (2017). Steps toward participatory design of social robots: mutual learning with older adults with depression. In *Proceedings of the 2017 ACM/IEEE International Conference on Human-Ro-*

*bot Interaction, HRI'17*, March 6–9, 2017 (pp. 244–253). ACM Digital Library. DOI: 10.1145/2909824.3020237. 49

Lee, S-S., Theng, Y-L., and Goh, H-L. (2005). Creative information seeking Part I: a conceptual framework. *Aslib Proceedings*, 57(5), 460–475. DOI: 10.1108/00012530510621897.

Lee, J. Y. and Lim, J. Y. (2017). The prospect of the fourth industrial revolution and home health-care in super-aged society. *Annals of Geriatric Medicine and Research*, 21(3), 95–100. DOI: 10.4235/agmr.2017.21.3.95.

Lee, S. J. (2009). Spatializing English-literacy classrooms and third-space possibility: Classroom analyses based on teacher-student power relationships within a Korean secondary-school context. (Unpublished doctoral dissertation). University at Buffalo, State University of New York, U.S. https://ubir.buffalo.edu/xmlui/handle/10477/45477 (Archived by Web-Cite® at http://www.webcitation.org/6xuQS7dqN). 39

Lefebvre, H. (1991). *The Production of Space* (D. Nicholson-Smith, Trans.). Blackwell. 34

Leigh Star, S. (2010). This is not a boundary object: reflections on the origin of a concept. *Science, Technology, and Human Values*, 35(5), 601–617. DOI: 10.1177/0162243910377624. 8

Li, X., Chen, W., Zhou, Y., Athalye, S., Chin, W., Kit, R., Setiawan, V., and Hansen P. (2019). Mobile phone-based device for personalised tutorials of 3D printer assembly. In M. Kurosu (Ed.), *Human–Computer Interaction. Recognition and Interaction Technologies* (pp. 37–48). Springer. (Lecture Notes in Computer Science, 11567). DOI: 10.1007/978-3-030-22643-5_4. 22, 85

Liley, S. (2012). The impact of cultural values on Maori information behavior. *Libri*, 62(4), 377-–388. DOI: 10.1515/libri-2012-0029. 59

Longo, B. (2014). R U there? Cell phones, participatory design, and intercultural dialogue. *IEEE Transactions on Professional Communication*, 57(3), 204–215. DOI: 10.1109/TPC.2014.2341437. 47, 49, 56

Lou, X., Li, X., Hansen, P., and Du, P. (2020a). Hand-adaptive user interface: improved gestural in-teraction in virtual reality. *Virtual Reality*, 1–19. DOI: 10.1007/s10055-020-00461-7. 85

Lou, X., Li, X., Hansen, P, and Peng, Z. (2020b). An empirical evaluation on arm fatigue in free hand interaction and guidelines for designing natural user interfaces in VR. (LNCS). In *Proceedings of the International Conference on Human–Computer Interaction* (pp. 313–324). Springer. (Lecture Notes in Computer Science, 12190). DOI: 10.1007/978-3-030-49695-1_21. 85

Lourens, M. (2013). An exploration of Xhosa speaking patients' understanding of cancer treatment and its influence on their treatment experience. *Journal of Psychosocial Oncology*, 31(1), 103–121. DOI: 10.1080/07347332.2012.741091. 86, 89

Luo, S., Wang, J., Xiao, Y. and Tong, D.Y.K. (2020). Two-path model of information sharing in new product development activities. *Information Development*, 36(3), 312–326. DOI: 10.1177/0266666919852398. 52

Lyng, K. M. and Pedersen, B. S. (2011). Participatory design for computerization of clinical practice guidelines. *Journal of Biomedical Informatics*, 44(5), 909–918. DOI: 10.1016/j.jbi.2011.05.005. 66

MacDonald, M. N. (2019). The discourse of 'thirdness' in intercultural studies. *Language and Intercultural Communication*, 19(1), 93–109. DOI: 10.1080/14708477.2019.1544788. 35

Maggio, T. (2018). The naked designer: changing the self. *Technoetic Arts*, 16(2), 221-230. DOI: 10.1386/tear.16.2.221_1. 60

Maher, M. L., Bilda, Z., and Gül, L. F. (2006). Impact of collaborative virtual environments on design behavior. In J.S. Gero (Ed.), *Design Computing and Cognition '06* (pp. 305–321). Springer. DOI: 10.1007/978-1-4020-5131-9_16. 40

Mäkelä, T. and Helfenstein, S. (2016). Developing a conceptual framework for participatory design of psychosocial and physical learning environments. *Learning Environments Research*, 19(3), 411–440. DOI: 10.1007/s10984-016-9214-9. 61

Makri, S. and Warwick, C. (2010). Information for inspiration: understanding architects' information seeking and use behaviors to inform design. *Journal of the American Society for Information Science and Technology*, 61(9), 1745–1770. DOI: 10.1002/asi.21338. 50

Manda, M. I. and Dhaou, S. B. (2019). Responding to the challenges and opportunities in the 4th Industrial revolution in developing countries. In S.B. Dhaou, L. Carter and M. Gregory (Eds.), *Proceedings of the 12th International Conference on Theory and Practice of Electronic Governance* (pp. 244–253). ACM Digital Library. DOI: 10.1145/3326365.3326398. 2

Maniotes, L. K. (2018). *Guided Inquiry Design® in Action: Elementary School*. ABC-CLIO, LLC. 36

Maniotes, L. K. (2005). The Transformative Power of Literary Third Space. Unpublished doctoral dissertation, University of Colorado at Boulder, U.S. xxii, 35, 36, 37, 46

Marchionini, G. (2008). Human-information interaction research and development. *Library and Information Science Research*, 30(3), 165–174. DOI: 10.1016/j.lisr.2008.07.001. 15, 16

Marchionini, G. (1995). *Information Seeking in Electronic Environments*. Cambridge University Press. DOI: 10.1017/CBO9780511626388. 13

Martin, J. (2006). Multiple intelligence theory, knowledge identification and trust. *Knowledge Management Research and Practice*, 4(3), 207–215. DOI: 10.1057/palgrave.kmrp.8500101. 60

Maynard, A. D. (2015). Navigating the fourth industrial revolution. *Nature Nanotechnology*, 10(12), 1005–1006. DOI: 10.1038/nnano.2015.286. 2

McCarthy, B. (1985). What 4Mat training teaches us about staff development. *Educational Leadership*, 42(7), 61–68. 57

McDonnell, J. (2009). Collaborative negotiation in design: a study of design conversations between architect and building users. *CoDesign*, 5(1), 35–50. DOI: 10.1080/15710880802492862. 47, 50

McDonough, S. (2014). Rewriting the script of mentoring pre-service teachers in third space: exploring tensions of loyalty, obligation and advocacy. *Studying Teacher Education*, 10(3), 210–221. DOI: 10.1080/17425964.2014.949658. 35

McIntyre, J. and Hobson, A. J. (2016). Supporting beginner teacher identity development: external mentors and the third space. *Research Papers in Education*, 31(2), 133–158. DOI: 10.1080/02671522.2015.1015438. 34

McIntyre-Mills, J. (2010). Participatory design for democracy and wellbeing: narrowing the gap between service outcomes and perceived needs. *Systemic Practice and Action Research*, 23(1), 21–45. DOI: 10.1007/s11213-009-9145-9. 49

McKenzie, P. J. (2004). Positioning theory and the negotiation of information needs in a clinical midwifery setting. *Journal of the American Society for Information Science and Technology*, 55(8), 685–694. DOI: 10.1002/asi.20002. 54

McKenzie, P. J. (2003). A model of information practices in accounts of everyday-life information seeking. *Journal of Documentation*, 59(1), 19–40. DOI: 10.1108/00220410310457993. 52, 54

Merkel, C. B., Xiao, L., Farooq, U., Ganoe, C. H., Lee, R., Carroll, J. M., and Rosson, M. B. (2004). Participatory design in community computing contexts: tales from the field. In *Proceedings of the Eighth Conference on Participatory Design: Artful Integration: Interweaving Media, Materials and Practices* (Vol. 1, pp. 1–10). CPSR. DOI: 10.1145/1011870.1011872. 40

Mesmer-Magnus, J. R. and DeChurch, L. A. (2009). Information sharing and team performance: a meta-analysis. *Journal of Applied Psychology*, 94(2), 535–546. DOI: 10.1037/a0013773. 55, 58

Meyer, A. (2016). Information behavior in academic spaces of creativity: a building science pseudo-makerspace. (MIT Mini Dissertation). University of Pretoria, Pretoria: http://hdl.handle,net/2263/65014. 38, 46

Meyer, A., Fourie, I., and Hansen, P (2020). A participatory design informed framework for information behavior studies. In *Proceedings of ISIC, the Information Behavior Conference, Pretoria, South Africa*, September 28–October 1, 2020. *Information Research*, 25(4), paper isic2004. Retrieved from http://InformationR.net/ir/25-4/isic2020/isic2004.html (Archived by the Internet Archive at https://bit.ly/3ngXl4k) (https://doi.org/10.47989/irisic2004 ). DOI: 10.47989/irisic2004. 2, 46, 52, 71, 76, 77, 83

Meyer, A., Hansen, P., and Fourie, I. (2018). Assessing the potential of third space to design a creative virtual academic space based on findings from information behavior. In *Proceedings of ISIC: The Information Behavior Conference, Krakow, Poland*, October 9–11: Part 1. *Information Research*, 23(4), paper isic1814. http://www.informationr.net/ir/23-4/isic2018/isic1814.html (Archived by WebCite® at http://www.webcitation.org/74FBUGQyU). xxi, xxii, 16, 39, 46, 49, 71

Meyer, H. W. J. (2009). The influence of information behavior on information sharing across cultural boundaries in development contexts. *Information Research*, 14(1), paper 393. http://informationr.net/ir/14-1/paper393.html (Archived by the Internet Archive at https://web.archive.org/web/20191103124823/http://informationr.net/ir/14-1/paper393.html). 59

Mitchell, J. S. and Vaughn, E. N. (Eds.). (2011). *Participatory Literacy Practices For P–12 Classrooms in the Digital Age*. IGI Global. 35

Mohammad Arif, A. S., Du, J. T., and Lee, I. (2015). Understanding tourists' collaborative information retrieval behavior to inform design. *Journal of the Association for Information Science and Technology*, 66(11), 2285–2303. DOI: 10.1002/asi.23319. 11

Moje, E. B., Ciechanowski, K. M., Kramer, K., Ellis, L., Carrillo, R., and Collazo, T. (2004). Working toward third space in content area literacy: an examination of everyday funds of knowledge and discourse. *Reading Research Quarterly*, 39(1), 38–70. DOI: 10.1598/RRQ.39.1.4. 39

Mor, Y. and Winters, N. (2008). Participatory design in open education: a workshop model for developing a pattern language. *Journal of Interactive Media in Education*, 2008(1), 12–28. DOI: 10.5334/2008-1. 50

Morisson, A. (2018). A typology of places in the knowledge economy: towards the fourth place. In F. Calabrò, L.D. Spina, and C. Bevilacqua (Eds.), *Proceedings of the International Symposium on New Metropolitan Perspectives* (pp. 444–451). Springer. DOI: 10.1007/978-3-319-92099-3_50. 85

Muller, M. and Druin, A. (2012). Participatory design: the third space in HCI. In J. Jacko (Ed.), *The Human–Computer Interaction Handbook* (3rd ed.) (pp. 1125–1154). Lawrence Erlbaum. DOI: 10.1201/b11963-57. xxi, xxii, 7, 8, 16, 17, 24, 33, 35, 40, 41, 49

Muller, M. J. (2007). Participatory design: the third space in HCI. In A. Sears, J.A. Jacko, and J.A. Jacko (Eds.), *The Human–Computer Interaction Handbook*. Fundamentals, Evolving Technologies and Emerging Applications (2nd ed.) (pp. 1061–1081). CRC Press. DOI: 10.1201/9781410615862. 39, 35, 40, 41

Nelson, J. A., Francis, S. A., Liverpool, J., Soogun, S., and Mofammere, N. (2010). Healers in a non-traditional role; a focus group study of Sangoma's knowledge of and attitudes to cervical cancer prevention and screening in Johannesburg, South Africa. *Sexual and Reproductive Healthcare*, 1(4), 195–196. DOI: https://doi.org/10.1016/j.srhc.2010.07.004.

Newman, K., Knight, S., Hansen, P., and Elbeshausen, S. (2015). Situating CIS: the importance of context in collaborative information seeking. In P. Hansen, C. Shah and C-P. Klas (Eds.), *Collaborative Information Seeking: Best Practices, New Domains and New Thoughts* (pp. 37–54). Springer. DOI: 10.1007/978-3-319-18988-8_3. 11

Nickpour, F., Dong, H., and Macredie, R. (2014). Information behavior in design: an information framework. *Proceedings of the 6th Information Design International Conference*, 1(2), 1390–1398. Blucher Design Proceedings. DOI: 10.5151/designpro-CIDI-130. xxi, 49

Nygaard, K. and Bergo, O. T. (1975). The trade unions—new users of research. *Personnel Review*, 4(2), 5–10. DOI: 10.1108/eb055278. 20

O'Day, V. and Jeffries, R. (1993). Orienteering in an information landscape: how information seekers get from here to there. In *Proceedings of the INTERACT '93 and CHI '93 Conference on Human Factors in Computing Systems* (CHI '93). Association for Computing Machinery, New York, NY, 438–445. DOI: 10.1145/169059.169365. 13

Olander, B. (2007). Information interaction among computer scientists. A longitudinal study. *Information Research*, 12(4), paper colis14. http://Informationr.net/ir/12-4/colis/colis14.html (Archived by the Internet Archive at https://web.archive.org/web/20190812094603/http://www.informationr.net/ir//12-4/colis/colis14.html). 14

Oldenburg, R. (1989). *The Great Good Place: Cafés, Coffee Shops, Community Centers, Beauty Parlors, General Stores, Bars, Hangouts, and How They Get You Through the Day*. Paragon House Publishers. 33, 34, 35, 43

Panahi, S., Watson, J. and Partridge, H. (2016). Information encountering on social media and tacit knowledge sharing. *Journal of Information Science*, 42(4), 539–550. DOI: 10.1177/0165551515598883. 52

Pane, D. (2007). Third space theory: reconceptualizing content literacy learning. In S.M. Nielsen and M.S. Plakhotnik (Eds.), *Proceedings of the Sixth Annual College of Education Research Conference: Urban and International Education Section* (pp. 78–83). Florida International University. http://citeseerx.ist.psu.edu/viewdoc/download?doi=10.1.1.426.353&rep=rep1&type=pdf (Archived by WebCite® at http://www.webcitation.org/6xuQYR5Ah). 39

Park, M. (2013). Multi-dimensional analysis of dynamic human information interaction. *Information Research*, 18(1), paper 566. http://informationr.net/ir/18-1/paper566.html (Archived by the Internet Archive at https://web.archive.org/web/20190812095300/http://www.informationr.net/ir//18-1/paper566.html). 14

Parsons, P. and Sedig, K. (2014). Adjustable properties of visual representations: improving the quality of human-information interaction. *Journal of the Association for Information Science and Technology*, 65(3), 455–482. DOI: 10.1002/asi.23002. 48

Parviainen, E., Lagerström, E., and Hansen, P. (2017). Composting as interior design—encouraging sustainability throughout a participatory design process. In *Proceedings of the 2017 ACM Conference Companion Publication on Designing Interactive Systems* (pp. 167–171). ACM Digital Library. DOI: 10.1145/3064857.3079139. xxii, 32, 56

Parviainen, E., Lagerstöm, E., and Hansen, P. (2016). Compost table—participatory design towards sustainability. In *Proceedings of the 30th International BCS Human Computer Interaction Conference* (pp. 1–3). BCS Learning and Development Ltd. DOI: 10.14236/ewic/HCI2016.63. 32

Pedell, S., Vetere, F., Miller, T., Howard, S., and Sterling, L. (2014). Tools for participation: intergenerational technology design for the home. *International Journal of Design*, 8(2), 1–14. 57

Pettigrew, K. E. (1999). Waiting for chiropody: contextual results from an ethnographic study of the information behavior among attendees at community clinics. *Information Processing & Management*, 35(6), 801–817. DOI: 10.1016/S0306-4573(99)00027-8. 35

Philbeck, T. and Davis, N. (2018). The fourth industrial revolution. *Journal of International Affairs*, 72(1), 17–22.

Pilerot, O. (2012). LIS research on information sharing activities – people, places, or information. *Journal of Documentation*, 68(4), 559–581. DOI: 10.1108/00220411211239110. 52

Postavaru, G. I. (2014). *A Participatory Research Approach: Designing Research with Vulnerable Women*. SAGE Publications Ltd. DOI: 10.4135/9781446273050013500202. xxi

Postelnicu, C. and Câlea, S. (2019). The fourth industrial revolution. Global risks, local challenges for employment. *Montenegrin Journal of Economics*, 15(2), 195–206. 2

Potter, J. and McDougall, J. (2017). *Digital Media, Culture and Education: Theorising Third Space Literacies*. Springer. DOI: 10.1057/978-1-137-55315-7. 39

Prekop, P. (2002). A qualitative study of collaborative information seeking. *Journal of Documentation*, 58(5), 533–547. DOI: 10.1108/00220410210441000. 13, 58

Presbitero, A. (2016). Cultural intelligence (CQ) in virtual, cross-cultural interactions: generalizability of measure and links to personality dimensions and task performance. *International Journal of Intercultural Relations*, 50, 29–38. DOI: 10.1016/j.ijintrel.2015.11.001. 60

Priya, R. S., Shabitha, P., and Radhakrishnan, S. (2020). Collaborative and participatory design approach in architectural design studios. *Social Sciences and Humanities Open*, 2(1), Article 100033. DOI: 10.1016/j.ssaho.2020.100033. 2

Punie, Y. (2007). Learning spaces: an ICT-enabled model of future learning in the knowledge-based society. *European Journal of Education*, 42(2), 185–199. DOI: 10.1111/j.1465-3435.2007.00302.x. 42

Purnell, D. (2015). Expanding Oldenburg: homes as third places. *Journal of Place Management and Development*, 8(1), 51–62. DOI: 10.1108/JPMD-03-2014-0006. 35

Reddy, M. C. and Jansen, B. J. (2008). A model for understanding collaborative information behavior in context: a study of two healthcare teams. *Information Processing and Management*, 44(1), 256–273. DOI: 10.1016/j.ipm.2006.12.010. 11, 53

Reddy, M. C., Jansen, B. J., and Spence, P. R. (2010). Collaborative information behavior: exploring collaboration and coordination during information seeking and retrieval activities. In J. Foster (Ed.), *Collaborative Information Behavior: User Engagement and Communication Sharing* (pp. 73–88). IGI Global. DOI: 10.4018/978-1-61520-797-8.ch005. 10, 11

Reddy, M. C. and Spence, P. R. (2008). Collaborative information seeking: a field study of a multidisciplinary patient care team. *Information Processing and Management*, 44(1), 242–255. DOI: 10.1016/j.ipm.2006.12.003. 11

Reynolds, R. and Hansen, P. (2018). Inter-disciplinary research on inquiry and learning: information and learning sciences perspectives. In *Proceedings of the 2018 Conference on Human Interaction and Retrieval* (pp. 289–292). ACM Digital Library. DOI: 10.1145/3176349.3176884. 23

Reynolds-Cuéllar, P. and Delgado Ramos, D. (2020). Community-based technology co-design: insights on participation, and the value of the "Co". In *Proceedings of the 16th Participatory Design Conference 2020 - Participation(s) Otherwise - Volume 1* (pp. 75–84). ACM Digital Library. DOI: 10.1145/3385010.3385030. 4

Richardson, S. and Asthana, S. (2005). Inter-agency information sharing in health and social care services: the role of professional culture. *British Journal of Social Work*, 36(4), 657–669. DOI: 10.1093/bjsw/bch257. 58

Rieh, S. Y., Collins-Thompson, K., Hansen, P., and Lee, H. J. (2016). Towards searching as a learning process: a review of current perspectives and future directions. *Journal of Information Science*, 42, 19–34. DOI: 10.1177/0165551515615841. 14

van Rijn, H., Bahk, Y., Stappers P., and Lee, K. P. (2006). Three factors for context-mapping in East Asia: trust, control and nunchi. *CoDesign*, 2(3), 157–177. DOI: 10.1080/15710880600900561. 23

Rittel, H. (1972). On the planning crisis: systems analysis of the 'first and second generations'. *Bedrifts Okonomen*, 8(1972), 390–396. 53

Robertson, T. and Simonsen, J. (2012). Participatory design: an introduction. In J. Simonsen and T. Robertson (Eds.), *Routledge International Handbook of Participatory Design* (pp. 1–17). Routledge. DOI: 10.4324/9780203108543. 20, 23

Robertson, T. and Wagner, I. (2012). Ethics: engagement, representation and politics-in-action. In J. Simonsen and T. Robertson (Eds.), *Routledge International Handbook of Participatory Design*. (pp. 64–85). New York: Routledge. 22

Robinson, K. (2009). *The Element: How Finding Your Passion Changes Everything*. Allen Lane.

Robson, A. and Robinson, L. (2013). Building of models of information behaviour: linking information seeking and communication. *Journal of Documentation*, 69(2), 169–193. DOI: 10.1108/00220411311300039. 52

Robson, A. and Robinson, L. (2015). The information seeking and communication model: a study of its practical application in healthcare. *Journal of Documentation*, 71(5), 1043–1069. DOI: 10.1108/JD-01-2015-0023. 52

Roegiest, A., Lipani, A., Beutel, A., Olteanu, A., Lucic, A., Stoica, A. A., Das, A., Biega, A., Voorn, B., Hauff, C., Spina, D., Lewis, D., Oard, D. W., Yilmaz, E., Hasibi, F., Kazai, G., McDonald, G., Haned, H., Ounis, I., van der Linden, I., Garcia-Gathright, J., Baan, J., Lau, K. N., Balog, K., de Rijke, M., Sayed, M., Panteli, M., Sanderson, M., Lease, M., Ekstrand, M. D., Lahoti, P., and Kamishima, T. (2019). FACTS-IR: fairness, accountability, confidentiality, transparency, and safety in information retrieval. *ACM SIGIR Forum*, 53(2), 20–43. DOI: 10.1145/3458553.3458556.

Rogerson, S. (2004). Aspects of social responsibility in the information society. In G. Doukidis, N. Mylonopoulos and N. Pouloudi (Eds.), *Social and Economic Transformation in the Digital Era* (pp. 31–46). IGI Global. DOI: 10.4018/978-1-59140-158-2.ch003. 5

Roschelle, J., Penuel, W. R., and Schechtman, N. (2006). Co-design of innovations with teachers: definition and dynamics. In *Proceedings of the 7th International Conference on Learning Sciences* (pp. 606–612). ACM Digital Library. 48

Rupčić, N. (2018). Intergenerational learning and knowledge transfer - challenges and opportunities. *The Learning Organization*, 25(2), 135–142. DOI: 10.1108/TLO-11-2017-0117. 2, 3

Salter, S. B. and Schulz, A. K. D. (2005). *Examining the Role of Culture and Acculturation in Information Sharing*. Emerald Group Publishing Limited. DOI: 10.1016/S1475-1488(04)08008-1. 50, 60

Salter, S. B., Schulz, A. K. D., Lewis, P. A., and Lopez, J. C. (2008). Otra empanada en la parilla: examining the role of culture and information sharing in Chile and Australia. *Journal of International Financial Management and Accounting*, 19(1), 57–72. DOI: 10.1111/j.1467-646X.2008.01016.x. 50

Sameshima, P., Slingerland, D., Wakewich, P., Morrisseau, K., and Zehbe, I. (2017). Growing well-being through community participatory arts: the anishinaabek cervical cancer screening study (ACCSS). In G. Barton and M. Baguley (Eds.), *The Palgrave Handbook of Global Arts Education* (pp. 399–416). Palgrave Macmillan. DOI: 10.1057/978-1-137-55585-4. 86

Sanders, E. (2013). Perspectives on participation in design. In C. Mareis, M. Held, and G. Joost (Eds.), *Wer gestaltet die Gastaltung. Tagungband DGTF-Jahertagung*, Transcript (pp. 65–79). Bielefeld. 12, 29

Sanders, E., Brandt, E., and Binder, T. (2010). A framework for organizing the tools and techniques of participatory design. In *Proceedings of the 11th Biennial Participatory Design Conference* (pp. 195–198). ACM Digital Library. DOI: 10.1145/1900441.1900476. 24

Sanders, E. B. N. (2006). Design serving people. In E. Salmi and L. Anusionwu (Eds.), *Cumulus Working Papers* (pp. 28–33). Copenhagen, University of Art and Design. 26

Sanders, E. B. N. and Stappers, P. J. (2014). Probes, toolkits and prototypes: three approaches to making in codesigning. *CoDesign*, 10(1), 5–14. DOI: 10.1080/15710882.2014.888183. 24, 28

Sanders, E. B. N. and Stappers, P. J. (2008). Co-creation and the new landscapes of design. *CoDesign*, 4(1), 5–18. DOI: 10.1080/15710880701875068. 24, 26

Sandu, A. (2017). Some considerations on the social construction of multiple intelligence. Appreciative intelligence. *Postmodern Openings*, 8(2), 22–39. DOI: 10.18662/po/2017.0802.02. 60

Saniuk, S., Grabowska, S., and Gajdzik, B. (2020). Social expectations and market changes in the context of developing the industry 4.0 concept. *Sustainability*, 12(4), 1362. DOI: 10.3390/su12041362.

Sarina, T. (2018). Enhancing knowledge management (KM) in the fourth industrial revolution era: the role of human resource systems. In J. Syed, P. A. Murray, D. Hislop, and Y. Mouzughi (Eds.), *The Palgrave Handbook of Knowledge Management* (pp. 411–435). Palgrave Macmillan. DOI: 10.1007/978-3-319-71434-9_17. 7

Savolainen, R. (2019). Modeling the interplay of information seeking and information sharing: a conceptual analysis. *Aslib Journal of Information Management*, 71(4), 518–534. DOI: 10.1108/AJIM-10-2018-0266. 52

Savolainen, R. (2017). Information sharing and knowledge sharing as communicative activities. *Information Research*, 22(3), paper 767. http://informationr.net/ir/22-3/paper767.html. (Archived by the Internet Archive at https://web.archive.org/web/20191225182834/http:// http://informationr.net/ir/22-3/paper767.html). 13, 52

Savolainen, R. (2016a). Approaches to socio-cultural barriers to information seeking. *Library and Information Science Research*, 38(1), 52–59. DOI: 10.1016/j.lisr.2016.01.007. 58

Savolainen, R. (2016b). Conceptual growth in integrated models for information behavior. *Journal of Documentation*, 72(4), 648–672. DOI: 10.1108/JDOC-09-2015-0114. 70

Savolainen, R. (2009). Small world and information grounds as contexts of information seeking and sharing. *Library & Information Science Research*, 31(1), 38–45. DOI: 10.1016/j.lisr.2008.10.007. 35

Savolainen, R. (2007). Information behavior and information practice: reviewing the "umbrella concepts" of information-seeking studies. *Library Quarterly*, 77(2), 109–132. DOI: 10.1086/517840. 53

Sawyer, K. (2012). *Explaining Creativity: The Science of Human Innovation*. (2nd ed.). Oxford University Press.

Scandurra, I., Hagglund, M., and Koch, S. (2008). From user needs to system specifications: multi-disciplinary thematic seminars as a collaborative design method for development of health information systems. *Journal of Biomedical Informatics*, 41(4), 557–569. DOI: 10.1016/j.jbi.2008.01.012. 52, 57, 61

Scariot, C.A., Heemann, A., and Padovani, S. (2012). Understanding the collaborative-participatory design. *Work*, 41(1), 2701–2705. DOI: 10.3233/WOR-2012-0656-2701. 7, 58

Schaap, B.F., Reidsma, P., Verhagen, J., Wolf, J., and Van Ittersum, M.K. (2013). Participatory design of farm level adaptation to climate risks in an arable region in The Netherlands. *European Journal of Agronomy*, 48, 30–42. DOI: 10.1016/j.eja.2013.02.004. 56,

Schuck, S., Kearney, M., and Burden, K. (2017). Exploring mobile learning in the third space. *Technology, Pedagogy and Education*, 26(2), 121–137. DOI: 10.1080/1475939X.2016.1230555. 8, 41

Schwab, K. (2017). *The Fourth Industrial Revolution*. Penguin. 1

Shah, C. (2017). *Social Information Seeking: Leveraging the Wisdom of the Crowd*. Springer. DOI: 10.1007/978-3-319-56756-3. 52

Shah, C. (2012). Coagmento: a case study in designing a user-centric collaborative information seeking system. In *Systems Science and Collaborative Information Systems: Theories, Practices and New Research* (pp. 242–257). IGI Global. DOI: 10.4018/978-1-61350-201-3.ch013. 49, 52

Shah, C. and Marchionini, G. (2010). Awareness in collaborative information seeking. *Journal of the American Society for Information Science and Technology*, 61(10), 1970–1986. DOI: 10.1002/asi.21379. 50

Shenton, A. K. (2010). Information capture: a key element in information behavior. *Library Review*, 59(8), 585–595. DOI: 10.1108/00242531011073119. 50

Shenton, A. K. (2007). Viewing information needs through a Johari window. *Reference Services Review*, 35(3), 487–496. DOI: 10.1108/00907320710774337. 52, 77, 89

Shenton, A. K. and Hay-Gibson, N. V. (2012). Information behavior meta-models. *Library Review*, 61(2), 92–109. DOI: 10.1108/00242531211220735. 70

Simonsen, J. and Hertzum, M. (2012). Sustained participatory design: extending the iterative approach. *Design Issues*, 28(3), 10–21. DOI: 10.1162/DESI_a_00158. xxii, 7, 50

Simonsen, J. and Robertson, T. (Eds.). (2012). *Routledge International Handbook of Participatory Design* (pp. 1–17). Routledge. DOI: 10.4324/9780203108543. xxi, xxii, 7, 41

Skattebol, J. and Arthur, L. M. (2014). Collaborative practitioner research: opening a third space for local knowledge production. *Asia Pacific Journal of Education*, 34(3), 351–365. DOI: 10.1080/02188791.2013.871690. 35

Skeels, M. M. (2010). *Sharing by Design: Understanding and Supporting Personal Health Information Sharing and Collaboration Within Social Networks*. University of Washington. 47, 49, 56

Soja, E. W. (1996). *Thirdspace: Journeys to Los Angeles and Other Real-and-imagined Places*. Blackwell. 34

Solomon, P. (1997a). Discovering information behavior in sense making. III. The person. *Journal of the American Society for Information Science*, 48(12), 1127–1138. DOI: 10.1002/(SICI)1097-4571(199712)48. 52

Solomon, P. (1997b). Discovering information behavior in sense making. II. The social. *Journal of the American Society for Information Science*, 48(12), 1109–1126. DOI: 10.1002/(SICI)1097-4571(199712)4. 52

Somerville, M. M. (2013). Digital age discoverability: a collaborative organizational approach. *Serials Review*, 39(4), 234–239. DOI: 10.1016/j.serrev.2013.10.006. 54

Somerville, M. M. and Howard, Z. (2010). Information in context: co-designing workplace structures and systems for organisational learning. *Information Research*, 15(4), paper 446. http://informationr.net/ir/15-4/paper446.html (Archived by the Internet Archive at https://web.archive.org/web/20190811050813/http://www.informationr.net/ir//15-4/paper446.html). 49, 50, 56, 61

Sonnenwald, D. H. (2006). Challenges in sharing information effectively: examples from command and control. *Information Research*, 11(4), paper 270. http://informationr.net/ir/11-4/paper270.html. (Archived by the Internet Archive at https://web.archive.org/web/20200506023629/http://www.informationr.net/ir/11-4/paper270.html). 13

Sonnenwald, D. H. and Pierce, L. G. (2000). Information behavior in dynamic group work contexts: interwoven situational awareness, dense social networks and contested collaboration in command and control. *Information Processing and Management* 36 (3), 461–479. DOI: 10.1016/S0306-4573(99)00039-4. 13

Spinuzzi, C. (2005). The methodology of participatory design. *Technical Communication*, 52(2), 163–174. 55

Stein, M., Boden, A., Hornung, D., and Wulf, V. (2016). Third spaces in the age of IoT: a study on participatory design of complex systems. In M. Garschall, T. Hamm, D. Hornung, C. Müller, K. Neureiter, M. Schorch, and L. van Velsen (Eds.), *International Reports on Socio-Informatics (IRSI)*, Proceedings of the COOP 2016 - Symposium on challenges and experiences in designing for an ageing society, 13(3), 69–76. 1, 4, 7

Steinerová, J. (2019). The societal impact of information behavior research on developing models of academic information ecologies. In *Proceedings of CoLIS, the Tenth International Conference on Conceptions of Library and Information Science*, Ljubljana, Slovenia, June 16–19. *Information Research*, 24(4), paper colis1905. http://InformationR.net/ir/24-4/colis/colis1905.html (Archived by the Internet Archive at https://web.archive.org/web/20191216153846/http://informationr.net/ir/24-4/colis/colis1905.html). 5, 6

Suchman, L. (2002). Located accountabilities in technology production. *Scandinavian Journal of Information Systems*, 14(2), 91–105. 40

Super, J. F., Li, P. S., Ishqaidef, G., and Guthrie, J. P. (2016). Group rewards, group composition and information sharing: a motivated information processing perspective. *Organizational Behavior and Human Decision Processes*, 134, 31–44. DOI: 10.1016/j.obhdp.2016.04.002. 58, 62

Tabak, E. and Willson, M. (2012). A nonlinear model of information sharing practices in academic communities. *Library & Information Science Research*, 34(2), 110-116. DOI: 10.1016/j.lisr.2011.11.002. 52

Tajvidi, M., Richard, M. O., Wang, Y., and Hajli, N. (2018). Brand co-creation through social commerce information sharing: the role of social media. *Journal of Business Research*, 121, 476–486. DOI: 10.1016/j.jbusres.2018.06.008. 8

Talja, S. (2002). Information sharing in academic communities: types and levels of collaboration in information seeking and use. *New Review of Information Behavior Research*, 3(1), 143–159. 13, 47

Talja, S. and Hansen, P. (2006). Information sharing. In A. Spink and C. Cole (Eds.), *New Directions in Human Information Behavior* (pp. 113–134). Springer. DOI: 10.1007/1-4020-3670-1_7. 10, 13, 51, 53

Talja, S. and McKenzie, P. J. (2007). Editors' introduction: special issue on discursive approaches to information seeking in context. *Library Quarterly*, 77(2), 97–108. DOI: 10.1086/517839. 54

Tang, T., Lim, M. E., Mansfield, E., McLachlan, A., and Quan, S. D. (2018). Clinician user involvement in the real world: designing an electronic tool to improve interprofessional communication and collaboration in a hospital setting. *International Journal of Medical Informatics*, 110, 90–97. DOI: 10.1016/j.ijmedinf.2017.11.011. 1

Tao, Y. and Tombros, A. (2017). How collaborators make sense of tasks together: a comparative analysis of collaborative sensemaking behavior in collaborative information-seeking tasks. *Journal of the Association for Information Science and Technology*, 68(3), 609–622. DOI: 10.1002/asi.23693. 48

Taylor, R. S. (1968). Question-negotiation and information seeking in libraries. *College and Research Libraries*, 29(3), 178-194. DOI: 10.5860/crl_29_03_178. 52, 77

Teal, G. and French, T. (2020). Spaces for participatory design innovation. In C. Del Gaudio, L. Parra-Agudelo, R. Clarke, J. Saad-Sulonen, A. Botero, F.C. Londoño, and P. Escandón (Eds.), *Proceedings of the 16th Participatory Design Conference 2020 - Participation(s) Otherwise - Volume 1* (pp. 64–74). ACM Digital Library. DOI: 10.1145/3385010.3385026. 23, 24

Thackara, J. (2000). Edge effects: the design challenge of the pervasive interface. In *Proceedings of the CHI'00 Extended Abstracts on Human Factors in Computing Systems* (pp. 199-200). ACM Digital Library. DOI: 10.1145/633292.633402. 40

Toma, C. and Butera, F. (2009). Hidden profiles and concealed information: strategic information sharing and use in group decision making. *Personality and Social Psychology Bulletin*, 35(6), 793–806. DOI: 10.1177/0146167209333176. 62

Toms, E. G. (2002). Information interaction: providing a framework for information architecture. *Journal of the American Society for Information Science and Technology*, 53(10), 855–862. DOI: 10.1002/asi.10094. 14

Torrens, G. E. and Newton, H. (2013). Getting the most from working with higher education: a review of methods used within a participatory design activity involving KS3 special school pupils and undergraduate and post-graduate industrial design students. *Design and Technology Education: An International Journal*, 18(1), 1360–1431. https://ojs.lboro.ac.uk/DATE/article/view/1800/1734 (Archived by the Internet Archive at https://web.archive.org/web/20190807171545/https://ojs.lboro.ac.uk/DATE/article/view/1800). 57

Tscheligi, M., Houde, S., Marcus, A., Mullet, K., Muller, M. J., and Kolli, R. (1995). Creative prototyping tools: what interaction designers really need to produce advanced user interface concepts. In *Proceedings of the CHI'95 Conference Companion on Human Factors in Computing Systems* (pp. 170–171). ACM Digital Library. DOI: 10.1145/223355.223485. 40

Twidale, M. B. and Hansen, P. (2019). Agile research. *First Monday*, 24(1). DOI: 10.5210/fm.v24i1.9424. 19

Twidale M. B., Nichols D. M., and Paice C. D. (1997). Browsing is a collaborative process. *Information Processing and Management*, 33(6), (pp. 761–783). DOI: 10.1016/S0306-4573(97)00040-X. 13

Uitdewilligen, S. and Waller, M. J. (2018). Information sharing and decision-making in multidisciplinary crisis management teams. *Journal of Organizational Behavior*, 39(6), 731–748. DOI: 10.1002/job.2301. 51, 62

Ujang, N. and Zakariya, K. (2015). The notion of place, place meaning and identity in urban regeneration. *Procedia—Social and Behavioral Sciences*, 170, 709–717. DOI: 10.1016/j.sbspro.2015.01.073. 3

Urick, M. J., Hollensbe, E. C., Masterson, S. S., and Lyons, S. T. (2017). Understanding and managing intergenerational conflict: an examination of influences and strategies. *Work, Aging and Retirement*, 3(2), 166–185. DOI: 10.1093/workar/waw009. 3

Vakkari, P. (1999). Task complexity, problem structure and information actions. Integrating studies on information seeking and retrieval. *Information Processing and Management*, 35(6), 819–837. DOI: 10.1016/S0306-4573(99)00028-X. 48, 58

Vakkari, P. (2008). Trends and approaches in information behavior research. *Information Research*, 13(4), paper 361. http://InformationR.net/ir/13-4/paper361.html (Archived by the Internet Archive at http://bit.ly/2Z0IXoc). 5

Valenzuela, A., Srivastava, J., and Lee, S. (2004). Cultural determinants of behavior in negotiations with incomplete information. In B.E. Kahn and M.F. Luce (Eds.), *Advances in Consumer Research* Volume 31 (pp. 493–494). Association for Consumer Research. 60

Van der Velden, M. and Mörtberg, C. (2015). Participatory design and design for values. In J. van den Hoven, P.E. Vermaas, and I. van de Poel (Eds.), *Handbook of Ethics, Values, and Technological Design: Sources, Theory, Values and Application Domains* (pp. 41–66). Springer. DOI: 10.1007/978-94-007-6970-0_33. 22, 23, 49

Van der Velden, M., Mörtberg, C., Van den Hoven, J., Vermaas, P.E., and Van de Poel, I. (2014). Participatory design and design for values. *Development*, 11(3), 215–236. 7

Verbaan, E. and Cox, A. M. (2014). Occupational sub-cultures, jurisdictional struggle and third space: theorising professional service responses to research data management. *The Journal of Academic Librarianship*, 40(3–4), 211–219. DOI: 10.1016/j.acalib.2014.02.008. 39

Vogels, E. A., Rainie, L., and Anderson, J. (2020). *Experts Predict More Digital Innovation By 2030 Aimed at Enhancing Democracy*. Pew Research Center [Online]. Available: https://www.pewresearch.org/internet/2020/06/30/experts-predict-more-digital-innovation-by-2030-aimed-at-enhancing-democracy/. 3

Vygotsky, L. S. (1978). Interaction between learning and development (M. Lopez Morillas, Trans). In M. Cole, V. John-Steiner, S. Scribner, and E. Souberman (Eds.), *Mind in Society: the Development of Higher Psychological Processes* (pp. 79–91). Harvard University Press. DOI: 10.2307/j.ctvjf9vz4.11. 36

Wagner, G. and Ikas, K. (2008). *Communicating in The Third Space: Routledge Research in Cultural and Media Studies Book 18*. Routledge. xxi, 62

Wang, H. (2007). Self-formation in a creative third space. *Studies in Philosophy and Education*, 26(4), 389–393. DOI: 10.1007/s11217-007-9036-4. 41

Wang, Y., Luo, S., Liu, S., Lu, Y., and Hansen, P. (2017). Crafting concrete as a material for enhancing meaningful interaction. In M. Kurosu (Ed.), *Proceedings of the 19th International Conference on Human–Computer Interaction. User Interface Design, Development and Mul-*

*timodality* (pp. 634–644). Springer. (Lecture Notes in Computer Science, 10271). DOI: 10.1007/978-3-319-58071-5_48. 32

Waterhouse, J., McLaughlin, C., McLellan, R., and Morgan, B. (2009). Communities of enquiry as a third space: exploring theory and practice. Paper presented at the British Educational Research Association Annual Conference, University of Manchester, England. https://www.educ.cam.ac.uk/research/projects/super/pubs.html. 45

Wenger, E. (1998). *Communities of Practice: Learning, Meaning and Identity.* Cambridge: Cambridge University Press. DOI: 10.1017/CBO9780511803932. 53

Westbrook, L. and Fourie, I. (2015). A feminist information engagement framework for gynecological cancer patients: the case of cervical cancer. *Journal of Documentation*, 71(4):752–774. DOI: 10.1108/JD-09-2014-0124. 86, 89

Widén-Wulff, G., Ek, S., Ginman, M., Perttilä, R., Södergård, P., and Tötterman, A. K. (2008). Information behavior meets social capital: a conceptual model. *Journal of Information Science*, 34(3), 346–355. DOI: 10.1177/0165551507084679. 58

Widén, G. and Hansen, P. (2012). Managing collaborative information sharing: bridging research on information culture and collaborative information behavior. *Information Research*, 17(4), paper 538. http://www.informationr.net/ir/17-4/paper538.html (Archived by the Internet Archive at https://web.archive.org/web/20190810190725/http://www.informationr.net/ir//17-4/paper538.html#.XtTxn0l7nIU). 51, 60

Williams, J. (2013). Boundary crossing and working in the third space: implications for a teacher educator's identity and practice. *Studying Teacher Education*, 9(2), 118–129. DOI: 10.1080/17425964.2013.808046. 7, 8

Wilson, R. (2019). Debate: information sharing is dead-long live information sharing! Current challenges and looking ahead. *Public Money and Management*, 39(5), 325–326. DOI: 10.1080/09540962.2019.1611234.

Wilson, T. D. (2010a). Fifty years of information behavior research. *Bulletin of the American Society for Information Science and Technology*, 36(3), 27–34. DOI: 10.1002/bult.2010.1720360308. 51, 52

Wilson, T. D. (2010b). Information sharing: an exploration of the literature and some propositions. *Information Research*, 15(4), paper 440. http://InformationR.net/ir/15-4/paper440.html (Archived by the Internet Archive at https://web.archive.org/web/20190806054958/http://www.informationr.net/ir/15-4/paper440.html). 51, 52

Wilson, T. D. (1999). Models in information behaviour research. *Journal of Documentation*, 55(3), 249–270. DOI: 10.1108/EUM0000000007145. 52

Wilson, T. D. (1997). Information behavior: an interdisciplinary perspective. *Information Processing and Management*, 33(4), 551–572. DOI: 10.1016/S0306-4573(97)00028-9. 51

Wilson, T. D. (1981). On user studies and information needs. *Journal of Documentation*, 37(1), 3–15. DOI: 10.1108/eb026702. 52

Wilson, T. D. (2018). The diffusion of information behavior research across disciplines. In *Proceedings of ISIC: The Information Behavior Conference*, Krakow, Poland, 9-11 October: Part 1. *Information Research*, 23(4), paper isic1801. http://InformationR.net/ir/23-4/isic2018/isic1801.html (Archived by WebCite® at http://www.webcitation.org/74IAnQkY8). 5, 6

Wipawayangkool, K. and Teng, J. T. C. (2016). Paths to tacit knowledge sharing: knowledge internalization and individual-task-technology fit. *Knowledge Management Research and Practice*, 14(3), 309–318. DOI: 10.1057/kmrp.2014.33. 49

Wohl, S. (2017). The Turkish tea garden: exploring a "third space" with cultural resonances. *Space and Culture*, 20(1), 56–67. DOI: 10.1177/1206331216646058. 7, 35

Wright, S. (2012). From "third place" to "third space": everyday political talk in non-political online spaces. *Javnost-the Public*, 19(3), 5–20. DOI: 10.1080/13183222.2012.11009088. 45

Xiao, J., Cao, M., Li, X., and Hansen, P. (2020). Assessing the effectiveness of the augmented reality courseware for starry sky exploration. *International Journal of Distance Education Technologies*, 18(1), 19–35. DOI: 10.4018/IJDET.2020010102. 85

Xu, M., David, J. M., and Kim, S. H. (2018). The fourth industrial revolution: opportunities and challenges. *International Journal of Financial Research*, 9(2), 90–95. DOI: 10.5430/ijfr.v9n2p90. 2, 19

Yasuoka, M., Nakatani, M., and Ohno, T. (2013). Towards a culturally independent participatory design method: fusing game elements into the design process. In *Proceedings of the 2013 International Conference on Culture and Computing* (pp. 92–97). IEEE. DOI: 10.1109/CultureComputing.2013.24. 12, 21

Ye, M., Hansen, P., Sigala, M., Du, J. T., Ashman, H., and Huang, S.S. (2019). Young Chinese tourists' motivations to engage in collaborative information behavior for group holidays. In *Proceedings of the 23rd Pacific Asia Conference on Information Systems (PACIS)* (Article 26). AIS eLibrary. https://aisel.aisnet.org/pacis2019/26/. 10, 11

Yeh, N. C. (2007). A framework for understanding culture and its relationship to information behavior: Taiwanese aborigines' information behavior. *Information Research*, 12(2) paper 303. http://informationr.net/ir/12-2/paper303.html (Archived by the Internet Archive at https://web.archive.org/web/20190806055511/http://www.informationr.net/ir/12-2/paper303.html). 55, 60

Zanotti, L. and Palomino-Schalscha, M. (2016). Taking different ways of knowing seriously: cross-cultural work as translations and multiplicity. *Sustainability Science*, 11(1), 139–152. DOI: 10.1007/s11625-015-031482-x. 55, 57, 59

Zaphiris, P. and Constantinou, P. (2007). Using participatory design in the development of a language learning tool. *Interactive Technology and Smart Education*, 4(2), 79–90. DOI: 10.1108/17415650780000305. 51, 55

Zedlacher, S., Khromova, A., Malinverni, E.S., and Hansen, P. (2019). Cybercities: mediated public open spaces - a matter of interaction and interfaces. In C. Smaniotto Costa, I.Š. Erjavec, T. Kenna and M. de Lange (Eds.), *CyberParks—The Interface Between People, Places and Technology* (pp. 25–37). Springer. (Lecture Notes in Computer Science, 11380). DOI: 10.1007/978-3-030-13417-4_3. 91

Zehbe, I., Wakewich, P., Wood, B., Sameshima, P., Banning, Y., Little, J., and on behalf of the ACCSS group. (2016). Engaging Canadian first nations women in cervical screening through education. *International Journal of Health Promotion and Education*, 54(5), 255–264. DOI: 10.1080/14635240.2016.1169942. 86

Zemits, B., Maypilama, L., Wild, K., Mitchell, A., and Rumbold, A. (2015). Moving beyond "health education": participatory filmmaking for cross-cultural health communication. *Health Communication*, 30(12), 1213–1222. DOI: 10.1080/10410236.2014.924792. 55, 57, 60

Zha, X. J., Yang, H. J., Yan, Y. L., Yan, G. X., Huang, C. S., and Liu, K. F. (2019). Exploring adaptive information sharing from the perspective of cognitive switching the moderating effect of task self-efficacy. *Aslib Journal of Information Management*, 71(4), 535–557. DOI: 10.1108/AJIM-07-2018-0176. 56, 57, 58, 62

Zhao, D. Z., Chen, M. Y., and Gong, Y. M. (2019). Strategic information sharing under revenue-sharing contract: explicit vs. tacit collusion in retailers. *Computers and Industrial Engineering*, 131, 99–114. DOI: 10.1016/j.cie.2019.03.035. 50

Zilahi, G. and O'Connor, E. (2019). Information sharing between intensive care and primary care after an episode of critical illness; a mixed methods analysis. *PLoS ONE*, 14(2), e0212438. DOI: 10.1371/journal.pone.0212438. 59, 61

# Authors' Biographies

**Dr. Preben Hansen**

Department of Computer and Systems Sciences, Stockholm University (Sweden)

preben@dsv.su.se

Preben Hansen is a Docent and Associate Professor at the Department of Computer and Systems Sciences, Stockholm University, Sweden. His main research focus is in the intersection of Human–Computer Interaction, Interaction Design, and Information Behavior. Preben's research focuses on the human in the center, interacting with the surroundings through various digital systems, services, objects and tools. His recent research deals with Gesture and distance-driven Interaction (with Dr Xiangdong LI) and Agile Research Methods (with Prof. Mike Twidale) and Collaborative Information Searching (with Dr Tina Du). He has published more than 120 academic articles/papers in journals and conferences and 3 edited books. He has served as chair at several ACM conferences like ACM CHIIR, ACM DIS, ACM/IEEE JCDL, TPDL and iConference. He has been a special issue editor for *Journal of Information Science on Searching as Learning* (2016) and special issue editor for *IEEE Computer on Collaborative Information Seeking* (2014).

**Dr. Ina Fourie**

Department of Information Science, University of Pretoria (South Africa)

ina.fourie@up.ac.za

Ina Fourie is a full professor and Head of Department of Information Science at the University of Pretoria. She is a rated South African researcher. Her main research focus is on information behavior, current awareness services, information literacy and autoethnography with special reference to cancer and palliative care and other existential contexts. She is a regular speaker and author in national and international contexts ranging from library and information science and education to healthcare. Ina serves on the editorial advisory boards of *Library Hi Tech*, *Online Information Review*, *Information Research*, and *The Bottom Up*. She was guest editor with Dr Heidi Julien of an *Aslib Journal of Information Management* special issue on Innovative Methods in Health Information Behavior Research (vol. 71 [6]: 693–702). Ina is currently Vice Chair of the ISIC (Information Seeking in Context) Steering Committee and part of the ASIS&T (Association for Information Science and Technology) Executive Board as Treasurer. She has published more than 130 articles, books and conference papers and has presented in more than 16 countries.

**Anika Meyer**
Department of Information Science, University of Pretoria (South Africa)
anika.meyer@up.ac.za

Anika Meyer is a Lecturer in the Department of Information Science, University of Pretoria. She completed her Master studies in 2016, titled: Information behavior in academic spaces of creativity: a building science pseudo-makerspace. She is currently enrolled for her doctoral studies at the Department of Information Science, University of Pretoria, titled: Information sharing in participatory design of a virtual academic creative space. Her research interests include creativity, collaborative information seeking (CIS), knowledge management, guided inquiry, third space, information literacy, information behavior and makerspaces—specifically the construction of these creative spaces through universal design, holistic ergonomics and participatory design. She has presented at international conferences (e.g., ISIC and EAHIL) and is a member of the ASIS&T African Chapter.

Printed in the United States
by Baker & Taylor Publisher Services